In Memory
of
Wm.   Thompson

HOW TO ORGANIZE
AND CONDUCT
FOOTBALL PRACTICE

Every man who knows how to read has it in his power to magnify himself, to multiply the ways in which he exists, to make his life full, significant and interesting.

—ALDOUS HUXLEY

HOW TO ORGANIZE
AND CONDUCT
FOOTBALL PRACTICE

By George A. Katchmer

Head Football Coach
State Teachers College
Millersville, Pennsylvania

Englewood Cliffs, N.J.
PRENTICE-HALL, INC.

PRINTED IN THE UNITED STATES OF AMERICA

42531—BC

DEDICATED TO

The 1953 Newport High School team, which won 17 consecutive football games—the finest high school team I ever coached,

and

The 1960 Millersville State College football team, whose 6-3 record made school history by setting a new scoring record of 187 points and an unprecedented third consecutive winning season— for unselfish dedication to the work at hand and team spirit that created a rare unity.

ACKNOWLEDGMENTS

The author extends special thanks to the following football coaches, whose contributions of practice schedules and ideas made possible a representative sampling from the junior high school through the large university levels:

COACH SAM THOMPSON, John Reynolds Junior High School, Lancaster, Pa.; COACH HOMER RICE, Highlands High School, Fort Thomas, Ky.; COACH DAVE HART, Johnstown High School, Johnstown, Pa.; COACH BEN MARTIN, Air Force Academy; COACH CHARLES "RIP" ENGLE, Penn State University; and COACH HUGH "DUFFY" DAUGHERTY, Michigan State University.

And to H. DALE SPAULDING and MRS. TRUDY ENGLISH for their assistance in typing the manuscript.

TABLE OF CONTENTS

3. **CONDITIONING AND TRAINING** (cont.)

ommended · The 880-yard run at the end of practice ·
Diet · Recommended pre-game meal · First aid tips ·
Half-time refreshments · Showers · Personal habits ·
Haircuts · Clothing · Vitamin pills · Sleep · Smoking
and drinking · Recommendation for the college athlete ·
Summer conditioning for high school boys · College sum-
mer training program · Some college demands · A rec-
ommended summer program · The running program ·
Defense depends upon top conditioning ·

Philosophy and objectives of junior high school football ·
Johnstown, Pa., junior high school program concepts ·
The Lancaster, Pa., John Reynolds Junior High School
program · Program starts with a letter to the parents—
simplicity keynote · Pre-season philosophy and organization · Presentation of practice programs · Outline of
junior high football procedure for a season ·

Geared to limited staff · Planning the small school practice · Plan practice with aid of staff · Plan must keep
players actively engaged · Plan must be carried out almost religiously · Specialities and off-field activities ·
The small high school pre-season practice plan · First
week · Second week · Third week ·

Large high school demands greater organization · Discretion a keynote · Sampling of a large high school program · Pre-season varsity football practice · Orientation
week · Staff organization · Staff meetings · Movies ·
Penalty period · Planning the practice schedule · Training rules · Daily routine schedule · Squad meeting procedures · Morning practice schedule · Afternoon practice schedule · Second week—practice schedule ·

HOW TO ORGANIZE
AND CONDUCT
FOOTBALL PRACTICE

1

THE IMPORTANCE OF PLANNING

Coach Is an Architect

Before any house is built, a plan or blueprint is first drawn up by an architect, from which springs the basic foundation upon which the house will be erected. The building will only be as good as its foundation. The same holds true for the success of a football team. Without a foundation based upon a well-planned, well-directed practice procedure, there can be little hope for even partial success. This foundation must be laid long before any squad member dons his practice gear. The architect of the football blueprint is the head coach. His success or failure will, in a large measure, depend upon the type of foundation he plans. As in the case of the house, the building starts from the basement, develops into the framework, and then the pieces fit into a strongly-built, sturdy structure. So the football squad with its new boys and veterans must be guided along a well-thought-out plan of action that will guide each boy along correct routine. It is a development plan much like a road map dictating to the players the journey that must be made, while at the same time it tells the coach where he and his retinue are at every stage of the trip. This road map is the itinerary which must be planned and executed by the head coach with the assistance of his staff and as complete fidelity as possible from his squad. It is not a guarantee for success, but it certainly will bring results over a period of time. The recognized architect leaves nothing to chance. A coach would be remiss to do so. While the architect deals with material things, the football coach is moulding human beings into a pattern that is measurable on any given game date. As a result, the coach must plan wisely and establish a foundation that will start at scratch and develop progressively to game readiness.

A Starting Point

In planning any practice schedule it has to be recognized that there must be a starting point. Where do you start? Ray Elliot, former coach at the University of Illinois, very aptly described such a beginning in a statement made at the Atlantic City National Football Clinic several years ago. According to Elliot, you assume the kids know nothing and you know everything. Start from scratch and develop your football program on a step by step basis, teaching the game to the newcomer and still motivate the veteran player in the form of a well-planned review. All of the fundamentals must be taught, skills developed, and conditioning must be achieved. The ultimate goal is team efficiency.

Development of the Practice Plan

From a common starting point your work and planning will be a race against time. As a result, time must be budgeted very wisely to insure complete coverage of every fundamental of the game. There can be no chance for oversight or omission. Every player must be purposefully busy. Interest and morale of your players will depend upon the planning put into the practice schedule. The effects of any laxity in your planning will be clearly demonstrated by your players.

Progress and Acceleration

Acceleration is the keynote of your practice strategy. You have on the average three weeks of practice before your first game. Football is no longer a simple game. There is more information to disseminate in a brief period of time than in possibly any other sport.

Once the starting point has been established, your practice must show development. Drills must be repeated to develop skills to their highest proficiency. New details must be unfolded on a progressive scale. Like the rungs of a ladder, a new step must be taken during each succeeding practice session. Certain objectives must be gained with the greatest conservation of time. You must know where you are going and what you want to accomplish. There are no short-cuts to success.

Football Is Taught in Pre-Season Practice

More than one veteran coach has stated over and over that you teach all of your football in the practice sessions prior to your opening game. Games are won and lost on the practice field. The basic fundamentals of the game are the prime objectives of the pre-season practice program. The ultimate goal is to have your team ready for the opening game. Once that happy day arrives, the coach merely becomes a director of personnel, cajoling, disciplining, correcting and motivating. His boys habitually unfold the skills of the game taught earlier according to their capabilities and the peak of condition they have achieved.

The Practice Plan Is Your Lesson Plan

Like the teacher in the classroom, the coach on the practice field must have some plan whereby he can chart the day by day progress of his squad. A practice plan is not the easiest lesson plan to draw on paper. The game today is a highly accelerated one engulfing intelligence, speed, brawn, skill and dexterity. It is a common practice in modern football to have at least one, and in many cases two, pre-season practice games. Such requirements dictate that a coach must have his squad in almost top physical condition and teach a comprehensive understanding of the basic factors of the game within an eight-day span, embracing a maximum of fifteen or sixteen practice sessions. The program emphasis calls for progressive drills plus accelerated teaching in blackboard sessions and otherwise which will give even the totally inexperienced boy a general understanding of the game.

Plan Must Incorporate Position and Individual Differences

To make such a lesson plan is indeed a tedious chore. You must keep in mind the importance of such a lesson plan. You have eleven different positions to chart. You have to formulate the drills and the system to be used based upon the age, weight, experience, temperament, and morale of a group of individually different boys. You want it to be as pleasant as possible without losing sight of the seriousness of the work at hand. The assistant coaches must be consulted and their functions outlined.

Time Element Important

Finally the evaluation of the different drills, the conditioning, and the timing must be made according to a time schedule. The time element is probably the most important decisions you will have to make in drawing up your practice plan. You can become absorbed with one phase of the game to the expense of other equally important areas of the game. The apportioning of time for each activity can be the foundation of a successful or losing season. I once observed a coach administering over an hour of calisthenics in a two-hour practice period who could not understand why his kids lost every game but one. He over-emphasized conditioning at the expense of the other basic requirements of the game.

Practice Schedule Is a Guide

You must keep in mind that any plan you formulate is to be used as a guide. It must be elastic enough to make changes as the occasion may arise. The experience of your squad will in a large measure determine the elasticity of your plan. It should be strictly adhered to, however, once you start your activities on the field. The purpose of this book is to expose you to several practice schedules on various levels from the junior high school through the major college. It is emphasized again these schedules are merely guides to give you perhaps an idea or two in drawing up practice plans or improving the one you already have.

Employing the Lesson Plan

A. Methods Are Important

In concluding this chapter the method of disseminating the lesson plan must be treated. In your education and psychology courses at college you studied the learning process. Such knowledge stresses the importance of the methods you will utilize in teaching the game of football to your charges. That is exactly what you will be doing the first three weeks of practice. You can have the best practice schedule possible on paper, but it will only amount to a scrap of paper if you cannot transfer its major aims and objectives to your boys.

B. The Learning Process

Learning is defined as making new behavior responses as a result of old or new experiences. Football covers a wide multitude of information and physical activity. A coach cannot and should not try to teach each phase of football as a separate part, but rather treat all of the component elements as a single enterprise. In memorizing a poem it is not recommended that the person learn the poem by memorizing a line at a time. Rather he is encouraged to read and re-read the entire poem with understanding and concentration to gain a mental picture of the whole poem, after which the lines fall into place. So in football you expose your charges to old and new experiences daily. The old will serve as review and drill from which new interpretations will be made and behavior responses strengthened. It is true that at the most in many of the activities the participation of your boys will be limited by the time allotted to that particular activity. You will, in the main, be exposing the boys to that phase of the program. However, by repeating the activity in subsequent practice sessions you will not only be exposing the boys to the drill but also strengthening responses much as in the memorization of the poem.

C. Learning Takes Place

A comprehensive whole learning develops. It can be likened to a large wheel with its many spokes, each of which represents a certain area of football. When all of the spokes of the wheel fit into place from agility drills, reaction drills, conditioning, everyday drills, team combination drills, timing, agility, offense and defense your team has reached playing efficiency. Better learning takes place when activities are apportioned over a short space of time than when the same activities have unlimited time. The endurance, enthusiasm, and interest is best maintained over short periods of time. Then, too, you must remember that at the most practice sessions should be limited to a maximum of two hours. You could very easily apportion too much time to one activity at the expense of another. No one phase of football can be minimized since every fundamental part plays a significant role in the total picture. The time allotment can vary according to the activity. The point to remember is that it is a three week pre-season program which will allow for the proper development of each area of the game. It is surprising how the parts fit together even when it appears too little time is devoted to some activities. With the expansion of today's game it is readily noticeable that the participants have made the necessary learning adjustment to the acceleration demanded.

SUMMARY

The game of football today demands and merits proper organization. Perhaps the area where preparation is most needed is in the sphere of practice. Football is founded upon the drills and activities of practice time that make up the foundation of football. Any framework must be based upon some plan. The coach who does not organize his practice program according to time economy and an outline of the activities which must be taught will be remiss in his whole coaching venture. The plan, much like the lesson plan of the classroom, must serve as a guide which will chart the course of the program daily. It cannot be totally rigid yet must not allow for too much deviation or the plan will fall apart. It must encompass the total program based upon time allotment to the various activities and proper methods of teaching. You, as the coach, are the architect of a game that demands the molding of youth.

2

THE FOOTBALL MANUAL

Manual Is a Text

It was mentioned in Chapter 1 that football entails the dissemination of possibly more information by way of activities, drills and game knowledge than any other sport. Any device which will serve as a guide thereby saving a coach precious time and enabling him to do a more thorough coaching job should be welcomed. The football manual is such a device. It is a notebook that contains mimeographed sheets of football material prepared by the coach for distribution to each member of the squad. Such a booklet becomes the textbook for the team. Just as the classroom teacher uses a text for his course so the football coach is wise to use the football manual as the bible for his course. It is a guide much like the practice schedule which charts the entire journey of the football squad from the opening practice date to the final game of the season. It is the complete framework of the team founded upon the coach's philosophy and system. With the manual there is little chance for errors of omission. It becomes the coach's teaching aid and the players' source for reference.

Make-up of the Manual

Manuals are inexpensive to make depending, of course, upon the coach's taste for simplicity. Naturally a manual encased in a hard cover with fancy design and printing will be more eye-catching and appealing than a plain paperback notebook. If money is available in the budget the former type is endorsed. The coach with a limited budget only needs access to a mimeograph machine, stencils, a ruler, ballpoint pen and a typewriter. With this available material he can run off enough mimeographed information to complete anywhere from one hundred to two hundred manuals. Even the most conservative and thrift-minded administrator would not object to the cost encountered. A loose-leaf booklet of 8 by 11 inch paper, convenient to handle, is recommended.

Need for a Manual Justified

The manual is important to any coach from the standpoint of time economy, use as a guide, teaching aid, and reference source. It gives him a greater feeling of security in that he feels he has done an efficient job of organizing. There is little chance for omission of any particular phase of his football program. To the player it serves as a guide, reference source, and his football text. It gives him a feeling of confidence because it does serve the purposes listed in the preceding sentence. For the college senior it is his crutch to lean upon until he picks up the experience and wisdom to make his own manual. The importance of the manual serves its purpose by giving the player material with neatness of detail in diagrams plus clear and concise statements of standards, procedure, and explanations. The hand-drawn student notebook in most cases is a sloppy jumble of words, and hieroglyphics that is not readily understood by the player who composed the work. In most cases, it turns out to be an unattractive notebook that draws very little response from the player.

Manual Must Be Accepted as a Textbook

The football manual should be required at every chalk session. Since it is referred to as a text for the football curriculum, it should be given the same care and attention received by the classroom text book. Players must respect and covet the manual as another textbook.

Do's and Don'ts of a Manual

Too often the yearling coach, and quite often the veteran coach, get carried away in their enthusiasm for detail and end with a notebook of voluminous proportions. I have seen several high school manuals that were entirely out of proportion in content. They were too detailed on everything from stances, steps, body balance, drills, etc. This, I believe, has a tendency to discourage a player rather than encourage him. Such a manual is advocated for the coach and his assistants. The player should receive a summarized version. Details should be taught on the field of practice. For example, linemen learning pulling out tactics don't have to have it spelled out in writing. They will learn it with lasting effect through drill on the practice field.

Since more and more coaches are becoming advocates of the football manual as a teaching device perhaps some do's and don'ts can serve as a guide and a caution in editing such a notebook.

DON'T

1. Get carried away with detail.
2. Over-slogan the manual.
3. Get too prolific on attitude and spirit (a few concise straight to the point lines will carry more potency than several paragraphs).
4. Let the players draw diagrams. Many people believe there is a transfer of learning value in such procedures. It is true, however, in most cases the game teaches itself under guidance and practice.
5. Set rules that will hurt you and the squad by their enforcement.
6. Include all of your drills in charted form.
7. Dwell on administration and procedure to any length in print.

DO

1. Summarize the manual as much as possible without curtailing intent or objectives. The coach should have a detailed manual to keep his philosophy and system as up-to-date as possible.
2. Make it adaptable—Allow for revisions.

3. Make it easy to understand.

4. Make it as attractive as possible under your circumstances: Such make-up can be done in many cases with the cooperation of the English class, typing class, and vocational department.

5. Use one good slogan at the top of each page.

6. List drills by names—Recognition will come with practice on the field.

7. Include the practice schedule.

8. Set your philosophy, standards, procedure, and system in simple yet emphatic detail.

9. Have all of the material ready for distribution during the first chalk session. It can be done in two ways, namely: (1) Distribute complete notebooks during this first meeting, or (2) Hand each player a loose-leaf cover and distribute the material daily as it will be covered on the field of practice during the pre-season drills. There is a lot of merit to this latter system.

10. Collect all notebooks at the end of the season.

ORGANIZATION OF THE MANUAL

The manual must be organized in a step-by-step manner. The following information is based upon the manual now in use at Millersville State College. Deleted for preservation of space are the offensive and defensive systems and other actual game mechanics such as punt coverage, kickoffs, pass numbering, etc. It may be added that the manual in use at Millersville is based upon information gathered from at least a half dozen manuals of successful high school coaches such as Harry E. Clarke, Reynoldsville High School, Dave Hart, Johnstown High School, magazine articles, books, and our own philosophy and system.

Cover

Term paper notebook is used. It is purchased from the college bookstore for thirty cents. The cover is paperback with a 2 by 3 inch celluloid window that reveals the name and title inscribed on the first page which is firm and glossy and part of the notebook. The make-up of the notebook is loose-leaf with each sheet kept firmly in place. In addition to the name and title of the first page the varsity and freshmen schedules are included but not visible through the celluloid window.

Pages 2 Through 15

Page 2 starts with and continues through page 15 with the rules, standards, and organization listed for the guidance of the players. These cover such points as: objectives, eligibility, academic requirements, financial aid, behavior in public and public places, travel procedure, use of language, dressing room deportment, punctuality, practice, earning of the varsity letter, taking care of equipment, blackboard sessions, pre-game, game and post-game instructions, staff organization, managers, training room procedure, insurance, and training rules.

Pages 16 Through 21

The types and mechanics of the Millersville State College multiple offense are summarized on pages 16 through 21. It could very well be your particular offense. To offer the reader an example of such a summary these portions of the manual will be included in this chapter. They may convey some ideas to the young coach attempting his first manual or even a suggestion or two to the veteran coach who may be in the process of revising his old one. Pages 20 and 21 summarize our rule blocking principles, and the three week pre-season practice schedule commences on page 22.

Seniors Keep Manual for Future Reference

The manual brought to your attention in this chapter covers perhaps more detail than would be recommended for the average high school manual; however, on the college level it is more than a manual in a sense. Since Millersville State College is a teacher-training institution, football becomes part of the curriculum from the standpoint of training for the coaching profession. As such the manual serves as a reference source for the graduating teacher-coach and becomes his personal property after his senior season of play.

Features of *The Millersville State College Manual*

The following excerpts from the manual in use at Millersville State College are published for your evaluation with the hope they may be of a suggestive nature that could offer an idea or two to the reader. Since the manual covers approximately 100 pages space prohibits its complete inclusion in this chapter. The information offered in this chapter would be peculiar to any manual on the high school or college level. Actual game mechanics and techniques omitted are those that fit our own particular philosophy and system which would not coincide with your ideas. However, your manual could follow the outline submitted in this chapter with substitution of your own ideas and system. With this in mind the Millersville manual covers the following essentials in the order submitted: the preseason practice schedule; practice schedule during the season; specific playing tips to linemen; special line and backfield drills; techniques of playing stunting linebackers; tips to quarterbacks; offensive field strategy chart with recommended plays for each division of the field; all phases of offensive and defensive strategy relative to punts, kickoff, and point-after-touchdown; pass areas and patterns; goal line plays; offensive plays; and finally the system and rules governing our multiple defense.

FOOTBALL MANUAL
MILLERSVILLE STATE COLLEGE

The Millersville State College football team is nicknamed the Marauders. The college colors are black and gold.

OBJECTIVES

Football at Millersville serves a four-fold purpose: (1) to aid the physical development of the participants; (2) to provide a fundamental background for students interested in coaching; (3) to provide opportunity for athletic participation on the mature college level; (4) to encourage recreation for the student body.

PHILOSOPHY

Athletic scholarships are not sponsored by the college, and hence there is no philosophy of "win at any cost." This is not to be construed to mean there is no emphasis on winning. Winning is the American way of life, and it is the measure of success in any endeavor. The coaching staff stresses winning at all times but not at any cost. It simply boils down to the fact that college football is rough and tough with the fun coming on Saturday in playing and winning that game. Everybody loves a winner. We strive to win through clean play and according to the rules of the game. Sportsmanship is stressed at all times. We try to win every game, but the losses are taken in stride. We try to profit from each loss by eliminating our mistakes in planning for the next game.

FINANCIAL AID

A teachers college education is about the least expensive available today, which is due to a certain amount of help provided by the state. A limited amount of work-aid jobs are available to the needy student. In turn students with scholastic difficulties are discouraged from accepting these jobs. Today it is difficult for the average or below average student to gain college acceptance. It is equally difficult to remain in college once accepted due to the competition to maintain high scholastic standards.

SCHOLASTIC STANDARDS

Millersville State College is proud of its scholastic standards. There can be no compromise with these standards. Student athletes get no special privileges. You must maintain the standards as set by the faculty or face dismissal from the college. Your education is the main show at Millersville and extra-curricular activities are the side-shows. You are coming to college for an education. Millersville will provide one of the best available. It is up to you to get the most from it according to your capabilities. You have a big transition to make from high school to college standards. In college the responsibility is strictly yours.

PLAYER CONDUCT

The coaching staff expects each player to conduct himself in a manner that will reflect the behavior of a scholar and gentleman in the classroom, in public and as a representative of the college. The latter requirement is highly stressed on trips, in

public places such as restaurants, hotels, etc., and as guests of
our various opponents. Such action is intended to eliminate
any horseplay, rowdyism, taking of souvenirs, etc., while repre-
senting the college. Dismissal from the squad can be the result
of such behavior. On trips each player is expected to make himself as comfortable as possible. He should get himself mentally
set for the game by reviewing his assignments and the scouting
report. Boisterous behavior, singing, and card playing will not
be tolerated. Every player will travel by the means of transportation provided by the athletic department. Each player will
return by the same means of transportation unless he receives
permission from the head coach to do otherwise. Permission is
granted only when members of the family are present and suitable arrangements are made to take care of his equipment.

ELIGIBILITY

Athletes at Millersville State are eligible to play four years of
varsity competition. Freshmen are eligible for all varsity teams.
Transfer students are ineligible for one full academic year,
which does not include junior college or part-time college-
sponsored centers. Transfer students are eligible to play jayvee
football. All freshmen and sophomores who do not make the
varsity team play with the jayvee team to gain experience and
playing maturity.

VARSITY LETTER AWARD

Varsity letters are awarded to those players who complete the
season and engage in at least one-half of the total quarters
played. There are some exceptions to this rule, usually based
on the discretion of the coach. Injured varsity players automatically qualify for varsity letters. Varsity club membership
is open to all letter winners. The varsity blazer is awarded to
Varsity Club members who earn three consecutive letters.
Players who complete four years on the squad without earning
a letter are awarded the same at the end of their senior year.
Managers qualify for a varsity letter at the end of their second
year of service.

CONSIDERATION TO MANAGERS

Football managing is a difficult and time-consuming task. As a result good managers are hard to find. The work is purely voluntary. We expect our players to be very considerate in their attitudes and demands on our managers. We would appreciate any little help you can extend that will make some of the countless chores expected from the managers less of a burden. The managers come under the jurisdiction of the equipment custodian. In turn a senior manager directs and assigns all managerial duties.

EQUIPMENT

Equipment has become an expensive problem to the athletic department. Every player will be solely responsible for all equipment issued to him. He *must pay* for any equipment lost or stolen if improperly handled by the responsible owner. Millersville State provides the best equipment money can buy. We can point with pride to our teams as the best-dressed in the country.

PLAYER INSURANCE

For protection of our athletes the athletic department insures every player, provides a team physician, a group of trainers, and a well equipped training room. All injuries must be reported to members of the coaching staff. Doctors will be consulted upon the advice and direction of the head trainer, head coach, or athletic director, Dr. Raymond J. Runkle. Do not go to a doctor without permission. All injuries should be reported. Often a minor injury can become a major one. Protect yourself.

TRAINING ROOM

Because of the pressure on the trainers prior to practice time we ask all players requiring treatment and taping to report as early as possible for this service. We emphatically discourage and will not tolerate last minute rushes on the trainers by players who had sufficient time to get the work done earlier in the afternoon.

DISCIPLINE

Discipline will be emphasized by all members of the coaching staff. Our practice time is limited which makes it mandatory that we economize on the time available by getting as much work accomplished as possible. Positive results can only be consummated by the complete cooperation of all personnel. It demands punctuality. Plan your activities to insure being always a few minutes early. Such a procedure will prevent disciplinary action which could result in dismissal from the squad.

COURTESY

All players are expected to be courteous to the coaching staff at all times. Coaches will be addressed as "Mister" or "Coach." Any discourteous attitude or contradictory arguing will call for dismissal from the squad.

ESPRIT DE CORPS

We expect a rough, tough group of boys who can show a family type of esprit de corps. We will not tolerate fighting or animosity among our players. By the same token we do not want hotheads who may cost us a game or put us into serious trouble through an inexcusable penalty on the field. If you cannot control your temper, don't put on one of our uniforms. I don't want any of my players banished from a game for poor sportsmanship, discourtesy to an official, or for fighting. Winning the game is the primary objective. You cannot contribute towards victory by being eliminated from the game.

BULLETIN BOARD

A bulletin board is displayed at a place convenient to all personnel. You will be responsible for checking before and after practice. Team information and announcements will be disseminated from this source. The alert player is an informed player.

PRACTICE CONDUCT

Practice periods are the foundation of any successful team. What you do in practice is what you will do in a game. It is here that you impress the coaching staff. It is here that you convince the coaches that you want to play, that you can play, and that you should play. A positive attitude means that you will give maximum effort at all times. It means that you want to be the first on the field and the last to leave. You cannot impress the coaches by trying to slack off, by being late, or by trying to avoid any rough work. Football is a physical contact sport which should be entered into with enthusiasm. Otherwise you should choose another less strenuous game—ping pong, for example.

Due to our limited practice time of one hour, we will demand maximum effort at all times. Any loafing or tom-foolery will bring disciplinary action.

Conduct of Specialists and Early Arrivals

All specialists, i.e., kickers, passers, punter, etc., will be expected to put in at a minimum 15 minutes prior to practice or after practice every day.

All players reporting to the field will go to areas designated by their respective coaches to work on eliminating deficiencies. Gathering in little groups to have a chat, or exchanging gossip prior to the call for formal practice will be strictly frowned upon. Neither do we want individuals practicing skills which they will not perform in a game. You have special skills called for by your position. Improve these skills. When the whistle blows for formal practice all work will be prescribed by the head coach's schedule.

Scrimmage Day

Normally all scrimmages will be held on Wednesdays. These scrimmages will play a major part in picking Saturday's starting line-up. Desire and perseverance usually brings recognition and success.

Pre-Game Requisites

Pre-game practice will be outlined by the respective coaches. Linemen will report to the line coach, backs to the backfield coach. The team will dress one hour prior to game time. Taping will commence at least three hours before game time. The team will be ready for final instructions by the coaching staff 40 minutes before reporting out on the field. The team will be led by the co-captains who will circle the field and conduct five minutes of warm-up calisthenics after which you report to your respective coaches. Specialists will go to designated areas of the field to practice their specialities. The last ten minutes of pre-game practice will be utilized in full team hand-offs up and down the field to get the feel of the game. The whole squad will retreat to the bench to await the captains' return from meeting with the officials. Helmets will be worn by the starting line-up. Last minute instructions will be given by the head coach after which the team will position itself on the field for the start of the game.

BENCH ORGANIZATION

Reserves will sit on the bench according to position, i.e., all ends, all tackles, all guards, and all centers on one side then all halfbacks and all fullbacks on the other side. The quarterbacks will sit in the middle of the bench separating linemen and backs in order to be available for information from each source and also to be easily available to the head coach.

HALF-TIME PROCEDURE

The half-time procedure will be scheduled in minute allotments. The rules provide a 15 minute halftime intermission. The schedule is as follows:

3 minutes—report to dressing room—toilet requirements and first aid.

5 minutes—line coach and backfield coach make corrections and adjustments to their charges.

4 minutes—changes, instructions, and corrections by head coach.

3 minutes—report to field for warmup and second half play.

CONFERENCE MEMBERSHIP

Millersville State belongs to three collegiate organizations: the National Collegiate Athletic Association (NCAA), the National Association of Intercollegiate Athletics (NAIA), and the State Teachers College Conference. The rules of all three organizations govern our policies; however, the conference has adopted the playing rules of the NAIA which are similar to high school rules, to avoid confusion in transformation from high school to college play.

Personal Habits and Training Rules

In the matter of personal habits there are no strict and stringent rules. Certain recommendations are made which are intended for your welfare and to insure successful college tenure. We expect our football players to keep a healthy sleep cycle during the season. This suggests that you establish a definite bedtime which you will adhere to religiously. You should get the minimum of eight hours of sleep nightly. These eight hours will not be beneficial if you retire at different hours nightly. The night before a game we expect everyone in bed by 11:00 P.M.

In the matter of smoking it is to be recognized that smoking has become a national habit. Such recognition does not infer that the habit is a good one nor does it construe an endorsement. However, being realistic, the football policy is that you are permitted to smoke as long as it is in your room and not on the campus. It is recommended that you curtail the habit as much as possible.

The matter of drinking poses a similar problem. Many of you were probably permitted to drink at home. Our policy is to frown upon drinking during the football season. The policy of the college administration is to prohibit drinking and expulsion is the result of drunkenness on campus. The coaching staff will not act as police checking upon your actions; however, let it be clear to each of you that any signs of hang-over, etc., on the field, or being noticed in an intoxicated state will bring expulsion from the team.

Eating habits should also be established. The college plans and serves three meals daily which offer sufficient calories to maintain or even allow you to gain weight. The matter of eating between meals is not beneficial to you. A light snack before bedtime is endorsed.

The Football Staff and Delegated Duties

The athletic department is headed by Dr. Raymond J. Runkle who serves as head of the department of health and physical education in addition to duties as the director of athletics. Dr. Runkle handles all administrative and supervisory functions relative to athletics. He has complete authority over the various coaching staffs.

George A. Katchmer, head football coach, sets the football policy. He organizes the staff as to delegated powers and functions. He plans and establishes the system which includes offense and defense. He organizes the practice schedule, assigns scouts for observing the various opponents, aids in planning the football schedule, plans all chalk sessions, compiles the scouting reports, conducts the recruitment program, maintains public relations with the press, radio, and television, plans the budget, selects equipment, and carries out numerous other functions associated with the head coaching position. Because of the load of these many duties Coach Katchmer delegates all functional work on the field to his assistants.

The line coach, Eugene Groff, has complete charge of all line candidates. It is his job to have seven linemen ready to start the game on Saturday. He teaches all fundamentals associated with line play. He recommends the starting line and has complete charge of substituting linemen during the game.

Arthur Hulme, the backfield coach, carries out similar functions with the backs. He names the starting backfield and makes all substitutions.

The head coach will substitute all quarterbacks offensively. All other substitutes must report to Mr. Katchmer before entering the game. He may have instructions to be relayed to someone in the game. There are times when the head coach will substitute a lineman or a back at a particular stage of the game. Since the head coach is concerned with the over all offensive and defensive play of the team he depends upon his assistants to detect the flaws and make the corrections.

The line coach will also make defensive substitutions of all linebackers which will include fullbacks (or heavy backs used as linebackers). The backfield coach will substitute all backs including quarterbacks on defense.

The jayvee coaches will conduct their squads in a similar way for all scheduled games. During practice certain demands will be made upon them by the head coach which are aimed to benefit the varsity team; for example, a controlled scrimmage.

The purpose of this detailed preface to the football manual has been to orient you with the policies, objectives, and general procedure of the Millersville State College football team. It is hoped that you will be familiar with the policy and strive to make it work. It is also our hope that you will strive to be a player we can be proud to number among Marauder greats.

THE MILLERSVILLE FOOTBALL SYSTEM

MULTIPLE OFFENSE .... Includes *Wing-T, Straight-T, Split* or *Belly-T, Slot-T,* and *Single Wing*

DEFENSE .... Multiple

The addition of the SLOT-T to our Multiple Offense gives greater potential to the passing game. The slot-man adds another end to the attack. An automatic pass is possible at all times to the split-end.

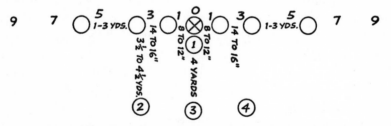

Fig. 1. Hole and Backfield Numbering

Hole number corresponds to inside shoulder of offensive lineman. The above diagram depicts our SPLIT or BELLY alignment. Hole numbering is the same for all other formations in our repertory of plays.

When an identical play is to be run to the left, the line will execute the maneuver by snaking out of the huddle and thus exchanging sides which keeps blocking assignments the same. Number 2 and 4 backs also exchange positions.

The center and quarterback will position themselves one yard in front of the huddle slightly to the left. In this manner the center can inform the quarterback of any line weaknesses which are relayed to him by the lineman. This eliminates confusion in the huddle. The quarterback gives the center the play and starting signal and turns to relay the same information to the huddle while the center positions himself over the ball. Backs can inform the quarterback of any possibilities before the huddle begins to form. There should be no talking in the huddle. The quarterback should call all plays quickly and with confident authority.

All plays are executed on "2" except automatics which immediately go on "1." As the season progresses staggered signals will be employed. Spread plays are automatically run on "1" while punts and place-kicks of any nature are executed on "HIKE." There are times when plays will be called on a silent prearranged signal in the huddle; on set; on set 1, 2, 3; on signals, etc. which demands that the team be mentally alert at all times.

In executing a play the Quarterback yells, "Set—1, 2, 3!" On this signal all linemen who had been in standing position, feet together, hands on knees, hop into their offensive positions. The Quarterback calls out the defensive alignment such as 44, 45, 53, 54, 62, 63, 71, 72, 83, etc. to alert his blockers. He then barks out his signals of "Hut 1, Hut 2." Thus: "Set 1, 2, 3 . . . 53 (5-3-2-1) . . . Signals! Hut 1, Hut 2." The team springs into action on the second hut. The Quarterback should snap off these commands.

On Automatics he simply calls "Change" then barks out three numbers. The first number is the new play—the second and third number are superfluous. Thus: "Change! 27, 33, 54." The play becomes "27" on automatic "Hut 1."

The first digit of a play refers to the back who will carry the ball. The second digit refers to the runway or hole.

Defenses are referred to as:

Odd 5-3-2-1, 7-1-2-1, 7-2-2, 9-2

Even 4-4-2-1, 4-5-2, 6-2-2, 8-3

Diamond ....Secondary with a safety man (5-3-2-1)

Box .... Secondary without a safety man (5-4-2, 6-3-2)

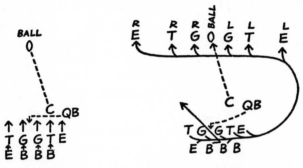

Fig. 2. Huddle   Fig. 3. Snake From Huddle

Wing-T (will be recognized when Right Half Flankers)

Quarterback will call play: "Hollenden Out-27 on 2." The play will be run as shown. Hollenden is the Right Half.

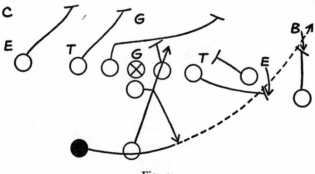

Fig. 4

Straight T

When the left half flankers the formation is a Straight-T. The Quarterback would identify the play call by, "Weber Out, 39 pitch-out on 2." Weber is the left half.

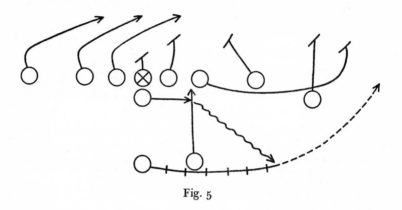

Fig. 5

To call these plays, to the left he would simply say, "Formation left, Weber out, 39 Pitch-out on 2."

Belly-T or Split-T (no back flankers)

Quarterback call play, "Belly 43 on 2."
The runner should always run behind the flow of his blockers.

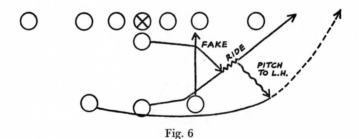

Fig. 6

Single Wing

Quarterback simply call, "Single Wing 47 on 2."
Wing man will help the outside tackle to double team the
defensive tackle unless he is playing in, in which case the
two tackles double team him and the wing man gets the
linebacker.

To avoid confusion on the appearance of many T-plays,
remember we are pulling the same play from three formations with no change on assignments. It gives the appearance of many plays and should cause the defense some
trouble.

We sometimes rely upon a spread formation for passing
especially when our pass pocket is poor on the sort formation. We use what we refer to as the Lebanon Valley Spread
and the Penn State Spread.

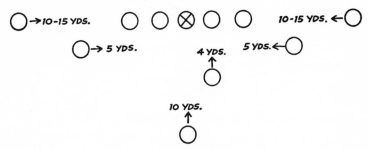

Fig. 7.   Lebanon Valley Spread

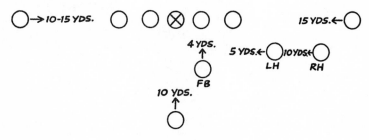

Fig. 8.   Double Slot

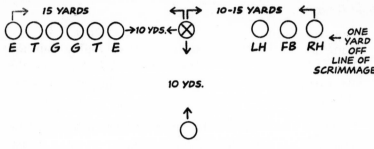

Fig. 9.   Penn State Spread

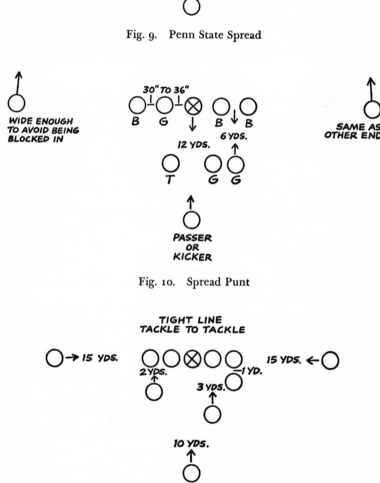

Fig. 10.   Spread Punt

Fig. 11.   Tight Punt

(The left footed kicker would have two blocking backs on the left side of the kicker.)

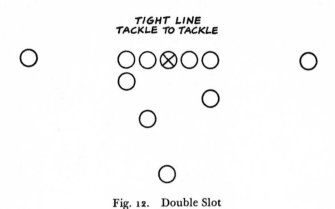

Fig. 12.   Double Slot

BLOCKING RULES

Numbering of Holes

Hole corresponds to inside shoulder of offensive linemen.

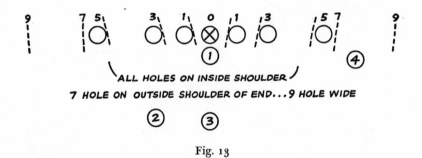

Fig. 13

Quarterback should never force a play against the strength of a defense. Use your automatics.

I.   On all *dive plays* men stationed at the runway will throw the essential blocks—All others release into the secondary. (On gap defenses—Wedge)

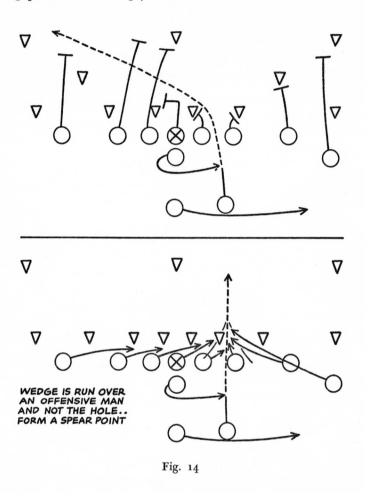

WEDGE IS RUN OVER
AN OFFENSIVE MAN
AND NOT THE HOLE..
FORM A SPEAR POINT

Fig. 14

II. On any play when no defensive man is stationed over you— release into the secondary towards the flow of the play. Middle linemen always clear the middle backer-ups. (NOTE: On even defenses, 4 or 6 man line, the center and two ends and sometimes tackles should be free to release into the secondary. Center should always take weak-side

backer-up. On Odd defenses, 5 man lines, the two guards
and two ends are always free to release into the secondary.)

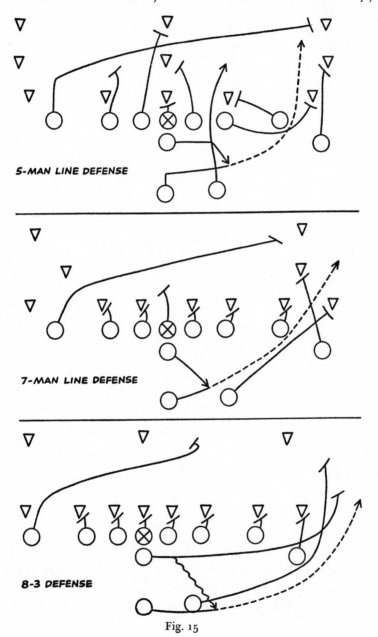

5-MAN LINE DEFENSE

7-MAN LINE DEFENSE

8-3 DEFENSE

Fig. 15

III. Against *seven and eight men lines* block one on one—
Allow the backfield blockers to take care of the extra linemen.

IV. *Against Gap 8.* On all 7 or 9 hole plays block the first man to your inside shoulder. Otherwise trap or wedge.

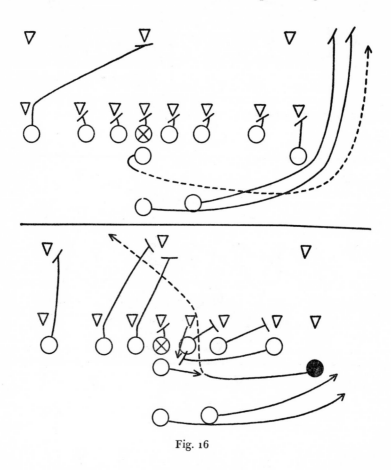

Fig. 16

V. On *trap plays*, linemen on the trap side double team the key defensive man. Others release into secondary. Offside men next to pulling linemen will compensate by hitting first man to their inside. When lineman pulls to lead a play and a man is over him, other linemen to the pulling side compensate by hitting the first man to their inside. Quite often a diving back will compensate by driving into the defensive man.

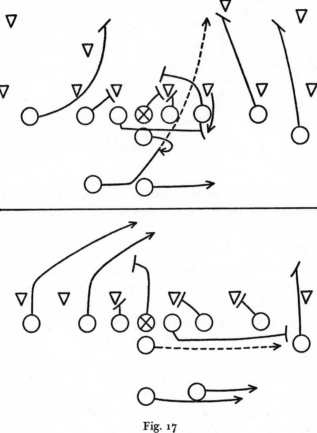

Fig. 17

VI. On *delayed or counter plays* the off-side linemen should throw a harassing block before releasing to the flow of the play.

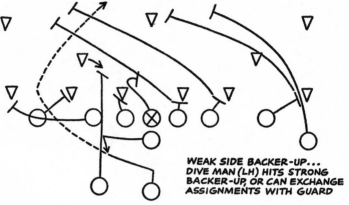

WEAK SIDE BACKER-UP...
DIVE MAN (LH) HITS STRONG
BACKER-UP, OR CAN EXCHANGE
ASSIGNMENTS WITH GUARD

Fig. 18

VII. On all 7 and 9 hole plays these rules apply for interior linemen and off-side linemen. Outside linemen observe the following blocking rules:

    7 Hole:

        End blocks first man on his inside shoulder

        Tackle—pull and hit first man on end's outside shoulder

        Flanker—hit linebacker (outside)

        Backs leading the play mop-up

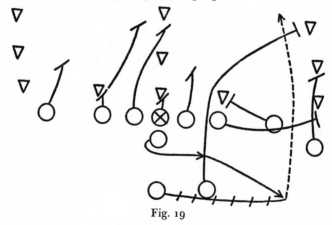

Fig. 19

9 Hole:

> End—same as 7 hole
> Tackle—block outside linebacker (by pulling)
> Flanker—block end or outside lineman in
> Leading backs—mop-up

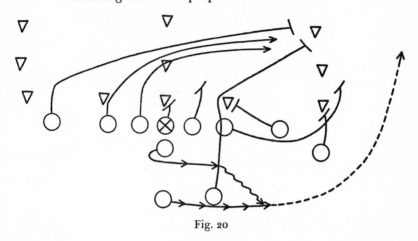

Fig. 20

SUMMARY

Football has made tremendous gains during the past decade. These gains can be attributed to over-all organization based in most cases on a well-defined football manual that covers completely each phase of the head coach's football philosophy. Just like the classroom teacher so the football coach must base his teaching material on a coherent plan outlined in every detail that will chart the course for a group of boys from the first day of practice through successive days of progressive work until peak efficiency is reached which will carry these same boys over their entire football schedule. This lesson plan is the football manual, a loose-leaf notebook of mimeographed material prepared by the coach for distribution to each member of the team. It becomes the text book for the football team. The manual offers little chance for errors of omission since it is the complete framework of the coach's philosophy and system. It becomes the coach's teaching aid and the players' source for study and reference.

3

CONDITIONING AND TRAINING

Conditioning, a Requisite for Success

Modern football can be styled as somewhat of a savage game of art, skill, and dexterity. It is one of the roughest and toughest games for American youth. A sport that prerequisites endurance, strength, and quickness.

Top physical condition is the criterion upon which the success of your team will rest. In the long run the well-conditioned team is the one that will cash in on the victories. Many an upset has been the result of thorough conditioning. Conditioning instills confidence. Confidence and a will to win are prime requisites for winning football. Therein lies the answer to a shocked sports world when a supposed underdog springs the big upset of the week. Actually the upset is not a fluke victory, but rather, the payoff to a well-planned training program. Conditioning and pre-season practice are synonymous; therefore, the first three weeks of football practice stress conditioning with the same emphasis devoted to other phases of the game.

Conditioning Influences Success

In 1954, my first year in collegiate coaching, I can truthfully state that our three victories that season were the result of out-conditioning our opponents. Talent-wise Millersville was lacking that season but the boys worked hard on conditioning. All three games were won in the last quarter. It was evident to our boys during the third quarter of each of these games that it would be just a matter of opening up in the last quarter. Each game ran true to form.

It goes without saying that many of you coaches can in a few minutes of reflection recall games that you won because of the degree of conditioning your boys enjoyed over a truly worthy opponent. Seeing a team come to life in the fourth quarter in an evenly matched game and cover over half of the field distance to score can only be attributed to long, well-planned conditioning sessions on the practice field. Perhaps no other acknowledgment can be more satisfying to a coach and his staff than the realization that victory was the result of team fitness.

Conditioning Takes Will Power

Conditioning is not a panacea that happens overnight. It is probably one of the greatest sacrifices a human being must make. To achieve good physical conditioning a boy must develop his self-discipline for the sacrifice he will be asked to make. He must steel himself to the torture of heat and sweat, the pain of tired, aching muscles, and the constant drive plus demand for more output. He has to develop a tenacity for physical punishment plus a perseverance to absorb the ordeals of the game. This cannot be accomplished without intestinal fortitude and will power. A will power instilled, guided, and abetted by the coach and his staff.

Carl Hetrick—An Example of Courage

If the lay public could only see a few examples of this raw courage, this perseverance, founded on a will power exhibited by these boys, they would watch the games with greater admiration for the contestants. How would they appraise a boy such as Carl Hetrick, who quarterbacked my Newport High School teams for four years? Carl had to undergo a cartilage operation prior to the 1952 season. This young boy lived football; he wanted to go to college and realized football was his avenue. The leg did not respond to exercises yet Carl reported for football. Neither I, nor my assistants, knew what hell this boy went through. He had threatened his teammates with a physical beat-

ing, if any of them exposed him to the coaching staff. He carried
pain pills to practice and did everything demanded from the
team by way of activities. We always ended practice with our
880-yard run at full speed and a 100-yard run up a steep hill
siding our field. Carl went up this hill in tears from the excru-
ciating pain, often on his hands and knees. He would not have
it otherwise. After the fifth game of the season the leg was
strengthened, and this young man led his teammates to a 6-4
log, earned All-Conference honors, and his team's most valuable player award.

Coach Is the Driving Force

Perhaps the greatest single trait developed in football is the
character of your boys. Good physical condition adds strength
to the character of a boy. Few of your boys can accomplish this
task alone. They need the sympathetic, yet the firm guiding
hand of a mature person. This individual is you and your staff.

It is the head coach who must chart the course. You have one
of the greatest jobs of salesmanship you will ever undertake.
You must sell each player of your squad on the value of top
physical conditioning. Too many players, both high school and
college caliber, cannot see the need of extensive physical training. They can only see the game and its excitement. The majority tend to rationalize claiming they are in top physical
shape and even during fatigue will not confess being out-of-
condition.

You must instill into each boy a pride for physical attain-
ment. You have to drive them and develop within them the
self-discipline to push themselves. This is no easy task, but it
can be done rather easily and quite successfully on the high
school level. Through the example of yourself, certain leaders
on your squad, national heroes, and a direct appeal to their
pride boys can be directed into channels chartered for them.
As boys grow older they change towards more independence,
but the high school boy can be molded into almost any pattern
by the wise coach. The challenge is greater on the mature college level, but here pride is a more potent motivating force.
The high school boy follows his coach almost blindly with trust

while the college boys want explanations and reasons for the demands upon their exertion. My own psychology of coaching and discipline has undergone a major overhauling in making the transition from high school to the college level.

Conditioning and Public Relations

Too few coaches are cognizant of the value a well-conditioned team can contribute to public relations. Probably one of the greatest tributes paid to me during my high school coaching career was one Saturday afternoon during the half-time intermission when a tall, scholarly looking gentleman stopped me at mid-field and introduced himself. He was one of Pennsylvania's highest ranking and most respected judges. He informed me that he had heard so much about the physical condition of my squad that he just had to drive to Newport to see the team perform. The judge, a former football great, honored me by saying it was the best conditioned and best drilled high school team he had ever witnessed. Needless to say, I passed this information to the team. It was not the first such compliment they had received, but it did add zest to their mania for training.

Newport High School

Such a reputation did not come during one season. The 1951, 1952, and 1953 seasons at Newport High School were the three most successful football teams of my coaching career. This success was founded with a group of boys that went through three seasons without a game-missing injury. In the last year, during an eleven game schedule, only one boy was knocked unconscious, and he was so remorseful over the incident he contracted a crying-jag that lasted hours. Physical conditioning was a fetishism with those boys. During time-outs they discussed the problems of the game in a circle while jogging in place. Believe it or not, practice seldom ran longer than sixty minutes, never beyond an hour and fifteen minutes. The conditioning program was based primarily on plenty of running centered on the 880-yard run at the end of practice and the run up and down the hill. This program will be discussed subsequently.

Over-Training Physically

Perhaps a point should be made clear at this stage of conditioning discourse. Don't train solely for the sake of conditioning in your squad. Many a team has been overtrained into a state of staleness from which it never did recover. Besides, conditioning alone will not produce a football team. Fundamentals of the game must be taught. A combination of both fundamentals and conditioning will produce successful football teams. Keep a definite plan at hand that will culminate in the development of all phases of the game. Don't over-emphasize one element to the detriment of the other. I can recall a certain coach who in a two-hour practice period administered 60 to 90 minutes of calisthenics daily to his squad and then couldn't understand why he lost every game.

INJURIES

Injuries Can Result From Fatigue

Injuries are quite often the result of over-fatigue. It is well to keep in mind that one tired player can be a harmful parasite to your team. Not only is he subject to injury, but his inability to cope with the responsibilities of his position is a contributing factor to a weakness in your squad which can only prove costly during the course of the game.

Injuries and Coaching Discretion

In the treatment of injuries a coach must practice the greatest discretion. It is only natural for certain boys to feint injuries or exaggerate the seriousness of an injury. They want to be fussed over, treated, or receive some satisfaction to their ego by recognizing some possible alarm in the coaching staff over any probable seriousness in his injury. Often it is a means that the star player uses to have his vanity flattered by the attention and kid-glove treatment he receives. It creates much consternation among his classmates. Conjectures are raised as to whether or not he will be able to play in the up-coming game. This is wine to many such boys.

The coach must be able to recognize such traits in his boys and deal with them immediately, or he will have a demoralized, dissenting team. You must handle the situation in your own way. Due to individual differences no one set recommendation can be advocated. Whatever you do, though, don't criticize or embarrass the boy in the presence of his teammates, although in some instances this has been the solution. It all depends upon the boy. Quite often his own teammates find subtle ways to snap the boy out of his desire for coddling treatment. Discourage it from the start or you will have a team of prima donnas.

Minimize Pseudo-Injuries With Pep Talks and Examples

Good little pep talks on toughness at the beginning of the season will become infectious. Use examples. Make up one or two good stories. You will be surprised at the effect it will have on your boys.

Here is an example of a story that can be used. You may tell of the average-sized boy who symbolized the toughness demanded by the game of football. In a particular game this boy (insert a name, etc.) was about to tackle a big fullback on a fourth and goal situation. Before he could make the tackle he was blocked across the backs of his legs. As he fell backward the snap of his breaking leg could be heard by the crowd. Rather than fall back screaming, he fell sideways towards the fullback and grabbed him by the ankle, thereby tripping him and stopping him short of the goal line. Only after the play was stopped did he acknowledge the hurt in his leg. The example just related is a true incident.

In your orientation talks inform your squad that boys with "guts" will win football games. It takes intestinal fortitude to play football. On the other hand, while you should minimize the moaning over a bruise or so, you must stress very emphatically that all injuries should be reported immediately after practice or a game. The minor injuries are quickly diagnosed as such and the boy informed as to the nature of the injury. A treatment is prescribed which he alone can administer. The more serious injuries should be referred to a trainer or physician. The wise coach does not want boys to hide injuries, be-

cause the sooner an injury is reported, the sooner it can be
cured, and the boy will be available for action. Serious injuries
should be treated completely, and no attempt should be made
to use an injured boy before he has completely recovered. He
can be crippled for life. No injured player can perform at maximum efficiency, while a healthy mediocre player will return
more results than an injured star. It is not uncommon to see
a boy performing in a game limping on a taped ankle or knee.
The game is not worth the risk.

Coach and His Training Methods

It is generally agreed that the coach is the man who must
push his charges towards reaching that stage of conditioning
which will produce peak efficiency. Even the person with the
necessary will power will find it easier to condition himself
under the direction of a leader. This does not infer that the
coach should set himself up as a Simon Legree who drives his
charges mercilessly and evaluates the degree of conditioning on
the number of boys who "pass-out" or vomit from the strenu-
ousness of the exercises. Too often such is the case. Many
coaches try to build a reputation for sternness and toughness.
This only shows a lack of professional training and understanding.

Conditioning Starts From Scratch

Any conditioning program should start at a stage of mildness
in exercise, running, and drills. The first day or so should be
spent in learning the conditioning program so that once the
pace is accelerated there will be little lost time as well as a less
amount of it needed. The work should be graduated, i.e., in-
creased in intensity daily.

The word mildness used in the preceding paragraph should
not be misconstrued to infer that the boys would have a lazy
time during the sessions. Quite the contrary, it must be inter-
preted that the workouts would be brisk, peppy, but short of
duration. Explaining the different exercises, drills, etc., will
consume most of the time the first two or three practice sessions.
The squad may go through a drill once to get the feel of it and

learn it, then on to another phase of conditioning. What they actually do perform should be at peak effort.

Training Must Be Graduated and Sold

Hard work should be entered into gradually, and the pace has to be stepped up daily. The boys should be encouraged day to day for it is during this stage of the training program that the quitting mortality is the greatest. The coach must use his wits. Any command of psychology should be utilized to its fullest. Pat the boys on the back; be sympathetic and understanding; congratulate them on their progress; tell them that it is tough and you know it; associate the need for it by game examples; create a spirit, an esprit de corps, that will be bought by the group. Kid them when necessary. Sometimes a good laugh will be the morale booster needed at a low ebb of training. There are countless ways of pushing your boys. Find ways as you gain experience. Get them from other coaches and use them fairly with understanding. Tell your boys that they can use their own bodies as criteria of their conditioning. If they do not feel stiff and sore the morning after the first three or four days of practice, then they were loafing. Stiffness and soreness are indications that they were working hard, that their bodies were not in the physical condition required by the game. If they continue to put forth maximum effort and gradually feel the stiffness and soreness leave, then they can measure the degree of physical shape they are achieving.

Weight Chart

The weight chart is another way of determining conditioning progress. A loss of several pounds of weight after a practice session is indicative of poor shape and perhaps overweight. A gradual decrease in this loss under maximum expenditure of physical energy until the loss is a normal expectance will indicate conditioning progress.

First Three Weeks Very Important

The first three weeks are the most important ones of the whole football season. It is in these weeks that you condition

your squad, teach them fundamentals, teach offense and defense, game strategy, and timing.

Hard work is the menu for the period. Conditioning underlies much of the program. It is in this stage that you handle the
heavy boy gradually so that at the end of three weeks you
haven't taken the spirit out of him. It is during these three
weeks that you don't overtrain the lean, wiry boy who needs
very little physical training. The coach will be wise to give the
squad a morning off about mid-week so that the heavy boy can
rest and the conditionally advanced boy has time to recoup his
enthusiasm and build a little reserve.

Conditioning Program

The actual conditioning program should stress running to its
maximum. There is no better method for conditioning than
running in one form or another, a recommendation stressed by
Chuck Medlar, veteran Penn State University trainer. Whether
it be wind sprints, short dashes or 100 yard dashes, the running
phase of training should be brisk or full speed at all times. The
jog-lap around the field is worthless unless it is done briskly
producing fatigue to a great extent. A fast 100-yard dash is
worth two slow laps around the field.

Calisthenics

While calisthenics have a warm-up value and do contribute
to good muscle tone, they should occupy only a small portion
of the training program. Thinking has changed radically relative to the value of calisthenics as measured against the time
consumed in their administration. Ten years ago it was not
uncommon to have thirty or more minutes of calisthenics in
each practice period. Today most trainers will inform you,
while not a waste of time, there are better methods calling for
less time. One of these is running which affects practically every
muscle in the body in one way or other. Others are agility and
reaction drills.

Calisthenics have their value during the first two weeks of
practice. A short peppy five minutes before every practice to
tone up tired, stiff muscles and a ten or fifteen minute session

at the end of practice with emphasis on heavy exercises (push-ups, wrestlers-bridge and others plus plenty of grass drills such as tumbling-somersaults, rolls, and burpees) is effective. The heavy drills should consummate practice, for to administer them at the beginning of practice only tends to fatigue muscles, thus diminishing any worthwhile participation with near maximum effort during the time allotted for fundamental drills.

Once the season starts the boys can take a few quick warm-up calisthenics such as the side-straddle hop, knee bending, and trunk-twisting exercises when they report on the field. This is done on their own initiative. While the above calisthenics program may appear controversial and debatable to some coaches, the general trend seems to lean in that direction.

Windsprints Recommended

It is the firm belief of many coaches and trainers that wind-sprints and dashes are the best media for physical conditioning. Short snappy dashes of five to ten yards at full speed not only conditions but teaches the boys to start fast and stop quick when the whistle is used stressing fast starts, speed, and hitting the ground again.

Dashes of 25, 50 and 100 yards and even 200 yards at full speed puts a heavy strain on a boy. It must bring results if continued daily.

It is suggested that, once the coaching staff feel the boys are nearing the peak of conditioning, every practice session could start with two 220-yard dashes or a total of 440 yards. The method is to dash the whole squad down and back equaling 220 yards, give them a slight blow of about 30 seconds, and then dash them down field and back. The complete drill consuming less than three minutes.

The 880 Yard Run at the End of Practice

Every practice session, except Friday, could end with what might be termed the 880 run. While still at Newport High School, due to the lack of time, this idea was incorporated into the practice schedule. The boys had to be kept in shape. Calisthenics or laps around the field would not serve the purpose.

The idea struck me that the boys should be able to run four dashes of 220 yards each with a little rest of 30, 40, 50 and 60 seconds between each dash. A little psychology was used in putting the idea over and a challenge issued to the team's pride. They were told that anyone who could run a half mile at full speed could hold his head up with pride because few high school boys could do it. This is not true, of course, but it is the core of the challenge. We already had the team finishing practice by running to the top of a hundred yard hill bordering the field and down again. The 880 would be in addition to the hill. Anyone that could not run the required yardage as prescribed would have to rest sufficiently and then run it. Stress team spirit and the importance of being in condition, if they want to have a successful season. With proper preparation the idea will catch on and the squad will take a pride in the chore. It is, in the opinion of many coaches who now use this medium, the best conditioning drill for keeping a squad in shape once the season starts. This 880-yard run is our conditioning salvation at Millersville. We have exactly one full hour of practice once classes begin. We keep our boys in condition with this five minute running drill.

Diet

[*Note:* The core of the following diet program is based upon facts gathered in a class, Athletic Conditioning And First Aid, conducted by Penn State University Trainer, Chuck Medlar.]

Diet plays a prominent part in every sport. At the beginning of the season during the first skull session a short discourse should be held on eating habits and foods. The high school coach has his problems in this respect. Many of his boys may come from low-income or emigrant families who may not measure foods according to vitamins or calories, but they serve plenty of meat and potatoes—often referred to as foods that stick to the ribs.

Frankly, the high school coach should not concern himself too much over this problem. As long as the kids are growing and adding some weight their diet must be sufficient. The main concern is that they get plenty of the food they are being served, and that it agrees with them. Some boys could digest a horse. Stress the importance of a big breakfast. There are scattered cases of malnutrition. The coach has a problem here which he must try to solve in his own way.

The one food you should stress is honey. It is a natural sugar. Most boys can get honey even in the homes mentioned earlier.

The ideal diet should consist of a moderate quantity of protein, an abundance of carbohydrates especially sugar, small (or sometimes moderate to large) amounts of fats and oils and plenty of vegetables, fruits and greens.

Rye, whole wheat, or corn bread is better than white bread in the diet.

Thinking has changed relative to desserts. They are permissible as long as they are not consumed at the morning and noon meals of the day of the game or prior to any practice.

Recommended Pre-Game Meal

For the high school coach the following recommendation can be made in regards to the pre-game meal. It must be recognized that the coach cannot dictate to parents as to the type of meal they should serve their boy. Quite often the boy is playing contrary to parental disapproval. Many of these boys play a game without any pre-game food. A mimeographed menu should, nevertheless, be sent to parents. In many cases a majority of the parents will respond to the recommendation.

The meal should be served at least three hours before the game. It should consist of a little orange juice or fruit cup; $1/2$ to $3/4$ pounds of medium-well done steak (or chicken, ham or roast beef); peas, red beets, or carrots; small baked potato with a pat of butter; two slices of toast with butter; fresh fruit or baked apple with lots of sugar; and hot tea or coffee. Under no circumstances allow milk. It takes too long to digest and will have a tendency to curdle under stress thereby causing gas in the stomach. Also avoid onions, turnips and cabbage as they will form gas.

Hubert Jack, Lock Haven State College Coach, employs a highly recommended pre-game meal. Under feasible conditions any coach would be wise to try it. Coach Jack gives his squad what he terms a big country breakfast at 9:30 A.M. It is the only meal his charges get prior to the game. They can eat all of the ham, sausage, bacon, eggs, cereal, etc. they desire. This allows 4½ hours for digestion. The kids are fed, relaxed, and ready for the game.

First Aid Tips

The use of sedatives for high school boys should be avoided, especially sleep-producing drugs.

Analgesic balm on the tongue about the size of a pea or bean will cut down on cotton mouth.

Liquid should be allowed in minimum to moderate amounts during practice. This is contrary to opinions of the past. The boys lose too much water and body salts during a practice session; thus a swallow and rinsing of the mouth will refresh the boy during practice.

Boys should be encouraged to use salt tablets before and after practice. Some boys may be allergic to salt tablets, i.e., they get sick in the stomach; therefore, these boys should season their food heavier than other boys.

Boys, that can, should be allowed to suck lemons during practice, since it tends to eliminate cotton-mouth.

Some coaches, especially major league baseball trainers, are experimenting with hot beef broth, bouillon, or consommé during practice sessions. Little paper cups are used. Anytime the athlete gets thirsty he can drink a cup of the hot clear soup. Advocates of this idea state that it does alleviate thirst and at the same time replenishes lost energy.

Chewing gum aids digestion and cuts down dry mouth and throat.

Glucose and dextrose tablets are good before a game and during half-time.

Half-Time Refreshments

Half-time refreshments cover a wide variety today. They vary according to the section of the country. Sugar cubes and dextrose, lemon and orange slices, hot tea, beef broth, ginger ale, and coca cola are the mainstays of half-time refreshments. More and more coaches are using Coca Cola. It has a sugar content, is cool (should not be ice cold, but chilled) and is refreshing. Ginger ale helps clear gas out of the stomach.

Showers

Showers are an important factor to take into consideration, because there is some difference of opinion about the water temperature. Each coach is entitled to his opinion. Many have experienced the different practices and have subjected various squads experimentally to each theory. From these various experiments one conclusion advocates that during the conditioning period, or the first three weeks of practice, there should be no hot water in the showers. The boys have expended a lot of energy on the practice field, and hot or warm water would only weaken them more.

As mentioned at the start of the paragraph about showers, there will be differences of opinion. Some coaches will be aghast at the idea of no warm water. How will the athlete cleanse himself with cold water, they will ask?

Cold water as it sounds is not recommended. The boys are asked to wait at least ten minutes, preferably fifteen, before they go into the showers thus reducing body temperatures. The water comes from the unheated water tank. It has been standing for several hours in the tank so has lost most of its chill. The water is comfortably cool and a good soap will wash dust plus perspiration from the body.

Boys can follow this up by going to a specially designated shower for a cold bath. This is optional; however, it may be found that very few will refuse the privilege.

The cool and cold showers leave the boys with an exhilarated feeling. It gives them a tingling sensation of coolness yet warmness. They feel as though they had had no practice at all.

Once the season gets underway, and the boys have reached a plateau for conditioning, the shower they take is optional. Warm water should be permissible. During October and November the coaching staff should insist upon a hot shower. The cool, not cold, one to follow is again optional to the boy. A short wait after the shower is recommended to allow the pores to close and the body to become acclimated to the atmosphere as a precaution against respiratory infection.

PERSONAL HABITS

Haircuts

The short, crew haircut is recommended by the coaching staff as a sanitary measure as well as "esprit de corps" for morale purposes. While not obligatory, you might stress it rather vigorously.

Clothing

As to clothing the staff can only recommend to the boys what they should wear. During the cold months of October and November check each boy before he leaves the locker room to see that he is properly dried and bundled-up. The importance of avoiding colds is highly emphasized.

Vitamin Pills

The coach, whose budget will permit, will be wise to keep all-purpose vitamin tablets available to his boys. They are well worth the money as an aid in combatting different respiratory virus.

Sleep

The matter of sleep is very important. It is to be recognized, though, that times have changed. Today boys have their own cars to ram around town. Television is another distraction. The coach has a problem. He must try to sell his boys in getting at least 8 to 9 hours of sleep nightly. If he succeeds, he will have an alert squad.

Smoking and Drinking

When it comes to habits such as smoking and possibly drinking there is little the author can recommend. It is a local problem and must be dealt with on a school and community level.

This book could probably list dozens of ways to handle the situation, yet none would probably fit your individual problem. About the only advice to be offered is that you be cautious; don't set hard and fast rules that will in turn hurt the squad and you.

Smoking, a national habit, is so much a part of our youth today, that any coach who is naive enough to think he can stamp it out is kidding only himself. The mode of living has changed over the past fifteen years. Don't misinterpret this statement to infer that the author endorses smoking among the athletes. Quite the contrary. Every fall one of the first lectures delivered is on personal habits. Kids should be sold on the idea of giving up smoking for the good of the team. It is a personal sacrifice for team improvement. Warn them, that, if caught, they will suffer the consequences. Have punishments for them, but do not dismiss them from the squad. If such were the case, probably as high as 50 per cent of the team might be cut.

I had the experience once of catching one of our junior high athletes, a seventh grader, smoking. His father being a personal friend, I felt he should know of his son's inclination towards smoking. After telling him, his remark was, quote: "Oh, that little son-of-a-gun! Do you know he was costing me a carton of cigarettes a week when he was in 5th grade?" Here was a proud father rather than one full of consternation over his son's ill habits. Such a case is not uncommon in American homes today. Can you set hard and fast rules? Yes, but you will only be hurting yourself in the end, since such cases are no longer scattered ones. Four or five laps after practice may not stop the habit, but they will wear off some of the effects of the cigarette and keep the boy in shape.

Recommendation for the College Athlete

A wise suggestion for college squads is to politely warn the players that, if they must smoke, the smoking should be done in their own room. On campus, or in public vicinity of the campus, smoking must be frowned upon and some repercussions must be the result. Warn the group that drinking usually brings expulsion by the college authorities. The coaches need not try to spy on the boys. You must be aware that with G.I.'s and married men on the squad there will be beer drinking, at least. The main concern is the condition of the men on the field; thus any man that drinks the night before a game or shows the effect of drink on the practice field ought to be automatically dismissed. Temperance and abstinence are to be advocated, but don't try to set hard and absolute rules of prohibition; this only invites deception. The boys or men will chance being caught. There are laws against murder, but murder is still being committed. The analogy between the two extremes is the same. Discretion is a virtue in treating abuses of smoking and drinking. Use it wisely; it may save a boy and a team.

Summer Conditioning for High School Boys

On the matter of summer training I have never asked my high school boys to condition themselves before reporting. While the point may be debatable I don't think this is a good idea due to the fact that young boys keep in shape by youthful aggressiveness. Getting a group of high school boys into top condition is not as difficult as it may appear. By the end of the first week most high school boys are in pretty good physical shape. There may be one or two exceptions such as the overweight boy or the awkward, immature boy, in which case individual programs should be drawn up for them.

During the summer ask the boys to spend about five to ten minutes daily on certain individual techniques such as improving their starts, speed for five to ten yards, cross-stepping, going sideways, pulling out, and skipping rope. Plan to have footballs available at the playground or baseball field. When a group of boys congregate at these spots, they can practice punting, passing, kick-offs and ball handling.

College Summer Training Program

On the college level summer training is more technical. Boys with deficiencies are expected to work on individual specialities and improve them. The punter is expected to practice punting all summer long; therefore, he must be given a ball and shoes for that purpose. The center should take home a ball and it is expected to come back well-worn. The quarterback also takes home a ball to improve upon his passing skill and ball handling. The halfbacks and ends have special skills to improve. The tackles and guards are expected to work on moving ahead and sideways, shiv and stutter, chicken fight, and work on agility. They ought to be given skip ropes and advised to use them daily. All the fellows are expected to work upon a fast start and improve their speed.

Some College Demands

Many coaches expect the college boys to return to the campus in the fall ready for scrimmage. Sometimes this is a necessity, and it is not poor coaching philosophy to scrimmage the first day of practice to see whether or not they have reported in condition. Many coaches decree that no boy can draw a uniform unless he can run a mile on the track course in six minutes or not many seconds over six minutes.

A Recommended Summer Program

During the month of August send each fellow a progressive conditioning chart which they are instructed to follow. When they report in the fall, start the conditioning from where their August chart had ended. Thus, if they were expected to end with 20 push-ups, 30 set-ups, 25 side-straddle hops, 10 drop-outs, 10 wrestlers bridges, 20 burpees, 10 six-inchers, and a medium fast mile, begin the first session with these same numbers and expect to increase them daily except for the mile which would be in the form of windsprints and dashes. It will be readily discernible as to who did and who did not follow your instructions. Such a program was recommended by Frank Leahy in 1950 at the Coatesville Clinic, now the National Clinic, conducted at Atlantic City, New Jersey.

The Running Program

To build up their running endurance the boys are instructed to start easy and gradually increase their pace according to the

outline of the chart sent to them. The first week each boy is
instructed to run a brisk 100 yards then walk the next 100 yards.
He repeats this four times for a total of 400 yards of brisk running and 400 yards of walking.

The second week he is asked to run alternately 500 and walk
500 yards; the third week 700 and 700 yards; the fourth week
he runs 200 yards at full speed and walks 100 yards. This is repeated four times. The fifth week he is asked to run 200 yards
and walk 50 yards and the number set at five times. The sixth
week he runs the mile for time each day. At the end of this six
week summer training schedule it is our belief that the boys
who followed it religiously will report in good physical condition.

Defense Depends Upon Top Conditioning

No team can play consistent, aggressive defensive football
without first attaining top physical condition. The physical
beating to the body from the standpoint of defensive football
puts high emphasis upon physical shape, perhaps more so than
that required for offensive football. The body must be alert at
all times and ready to respond to any offensive thrust. The
defense is at a disadvantage in that it is in the dark as to what
the offense might pull off. It has to guess or diagnose very
quickly. To do so it must be able to react almost intuitively.
This takes coordination and agility, two personal qualities attained only through thorough conditioning of the body.

SUMMARY

It all adds up to one conclusion, and that is that a mediocre
team can enjoy a measure of success providing it is in peak
physical condition. Top physical condition is a major requisite
for football in its broadest sense—offensive or defensive. It cannot be attained overnight. It requires great personal sacrifice
founded upon raw will power. Peak physical conditioning is a
great contributor to strengthening the character of a boy. The
coach and his staff are the guiding factors in directing the activities and motivating the boys on their squad. Conditioning is an

integral part of pre-season practice. It must be planned very carefully and observed at all stages of development to insure proper progress keeping individual differences in mind at all times. Training rules must also be drawn up with great discretion. Don't set hard and fast rules which can in the end hurt you and your squad.

4

THE JUNIOR HIGH PROGRAM

Philosophy and Objectives of Junior High School Football

Life is a continuous process, but with distinctive periods of development along the route to adulthood. Football can be analogous in direct comparison. The football player must develop in successive stages along the route to varsity participation. He goes from the embryo stage of young spectator then to the playground during his grade school days where he is exposed to the barest fundamentals of the game; namely, passing, receiving, kicking, and running the ball amid bullish, argumentative interpretations of the rules. There is no organization since the game continues after school in some lot which is the natural play instincts of the middle childhood period. While midget-midget programs are springing up all over the country, they cannot take the place or produce the positive results of a well-organized junior high program. The coach faced with the alternative of choosing between a junior high program and a jayvee team would, in my opinion, be wise to select the former for various reasons. Possibly the strongest reason is the fact that you can expose the kids to the game and set attitudes and desires at an earlier age, the formative, gregarious years.

The principal objective of a junior high program is to sell the game to a group of active young boys. Desires, attitudes, and skills are framed and nurtured during this stage of their development. Their appetites for football are whetted during this 13 to 15 age level by examples, movies, stirring pep talks, comparisons, praise, competition, and participation. This is truly the incubation stage from which develop smooth, highly skilled football machines. A love for the game is truly inbred at this level of development. Participation against competition is the keynote while emulation of varsity and higher level stars seems to be the natural output.

Johnstown, Pa., Junior High School Program Concepts

There are differences of opinion on the conducting of junior high programs as to length of practice, pre-season practice, amount of work to be covered, and other factors of the game; but the over-all picture tends to balance along, sane, acceptable, football concepts. Take for example, Dave Hart, successful Johnstown (Pa.) High School coach, whose organization covers even separate programs for the young, immature seventh graders. Dave feels that the seventh grade student is too immature to compete with eighth and ninth graders. He separates them into a program of their own to allow each boy to feel his way and make personal adjustments to the game on his own competitive level. As Dave comments, "Before we organized this program many seventh graders either quit or didn't come out for football. Now we have 150 out at the three schools with a full-time coach for each team. Each of the three junior high school teams has two coaches which adds up to a two-man staff at each school."

In essence the following will give a brief detailed picture of the Johnstown junior high school program. Practice starts one week after the commencement of varsity drills. During the first week of varsity practice all junior high mentors attend camp as varsity assistants. Meetings are held each evening with the complete staff during which time the varsity program is reviewed with each junior high coach. Each coach also receives a varsity football manual. After the season starts periodic meetings are held and all junior high coaches are assigned varsity scouting chores.

Plays are limited to two out of the five series employed by the varsity. Plays are limited—fundamentals greatly stressed. Defensively the teams are taught the basic five-man front stressing a 5-3 development which Hart believes teaches them better movements. Rotation is not taught in the deep secondary since it might tend to confuse the boys and cause them to lose confidence.

The junior highs practice twice a day for the first ten days, then settle down to once a day as school begins. Each coach regulates practice time limiting the length to two hours or less. Each school plays a seven game schedule completing the season during the last week of October.

The coaching staff at each of the junior highs teach the system and terminology of the varsity program. Drills, philosophy, and organization are also similar. It blossoms into a well-coordinated staff organization and over-all football program. Result? Dave Hart possesses possibly the best coaching record in Pennsylvania High School football competing in the tough Western Pennsylvania Interscholastic Athletic Association encompassing the large Pittsburgh area schools and the large steel and coal-mining cities. His 8 year record at Johnstown reads: 72 victories, 13 losses, and 2 ties; he has produced 3 undefeated teams.

The Lancaster, Pa., John Reynolds Junior High School Program

I have selected the three week pre-season practice program of veteran coach, Sam Thompson, of John Reynolds Junior High School, Lancaster, Pennsylvania, as a model practice schedule. Coach Thompson completed his sixteenth year at John Reynolds Junior High School with another undefeated team. In this span of years, Sam's record shows four undefeated teams, four Central Pennsylvania Junior High School Conference championships, and ten Lancaster city championships. His over-all won-lost-tie record shows a 59-36-8 log.

Program Starts With a Letter to the Parents— Simplicity Keynote

Thompson's entire program starts with a letter to the parents two weeks prior to the first practice session. His philosophy is simple, based upon the fundamentals of the game. In Sam's words, "We must start from scratch with these kids. Cripes! Some don't even know how to lace their shoes. We teach them how to dress and what part each piece of equipment plays in their personal protection. This eliminates the fear of being hurt. Facetiously, we explain the difference between a right foot and a left foot, then we teach step by step the fundamentals of the game through various individual or mass drills."

Pre-season Philosophy and Organization

Pre-season practice is limited to once daily in the morning with a maximum of two hours and fifteen minutes. Oftentimes specialists are required to report in the afternoons for a half hour session on their specialities. Regular season practice varies from one hour to two hours, with practice starting the first week in September; and a seven game schedule getting under way the third week of September. The coaching staff is composed of two men. The offense is centered around the T-formations with 12 basic plays while the defense is based upon the 5 and 6 man defenses. Evidence that the John Reynolds program is a highly contributive source in the overall Lancaster football picture is the emergence of Coach Boyd Sponaugle's McCaskey High School team as a real powerhouse in the tough Central Pennsylvania Football Conference over the last several years.

In the program that follows you will notice a lot of repetition. This is a requisite in a junior high practice plan.

Presentation of Practice Programs

There are several ways a practice plan can be organized such as the block by position plan as shown in Figure 1. The programs that will follow on the various school levels are presented in a sequence form because of compactness and coherent unity. In assembling the different practice schedules each coach submitting a practice plan had drawn them up in similar fashion. This coincided with my plans which leads me to believe that the majority of the coaches use this method. Any of the following programs can be adopted to the block style.

First Day:

Time	Centers	Guards and Tackles	Ends	QB and Backs
9:00-9:15	All ... Pass Drills ... Coaches Look for Coordinated Boys			
9:15-9:30	Whole Squad for Orientation Talk			
9:30-9:45	Whole Squad ... Calisthenics, Grass Drills, Agility Drills			
9:45-10:00	Wind Sprints	Wind Sprints	Wind Sprints	Wind Sprints
10:00-10:30	Stances	Stances	Stances	Stances
10:30-11:00	Coaches Explain Offense (Holes, etc.) and Defense			
11:00-11:10	Wind Sprints by Position			
	END OF PRACTICE			

Figure 1.   Block Style by Position Practice Plan

A three week Junior High pre-season practice program. (John Reynolds Junior High School, Lancaster, Pennsylvania)

Letter to the Parents

REYNOLDS JUNIOR HIGH SCHOOL—FOOTBALL

DATE:

TO THE PARENTS OF _____.

Your son has indicated a willingness to report for the varsity football team at Reynolds Junior High this fall.

We are happy that you have given your consent for him to participate in this sport. So that you can best understand the policy at the school, I am herewith setting down most of the important purposes and such.

First of all, this sport gives the coaches an opportunity to aid the boy to develop leadership, aggressiveness, team work, and development of the mind and body in such a way that I feel has no parallel with any other activity.

Discipline is a must. Good conduct, as well as a good scholastic standing, is required.

Promptness is required—this goes for attendance at school on time, and in reporting in time for practice.

Having many years experience in this coaching and teaching game, I can assure you that you will be more than pleased with the development of your son in many ways if he continues to remain on the squad the entire season.

We never dismiss a boy from the squad unless he cannot follow the rules and regulations set down, which we feel are not beyond his ability to do so.

Injuries do happen; you will be notified later as to the choice of treatment you may wish to pursue if such an accident should happen. Along that line, we have been very lucky in the past, in having few injuries; and this is due in most part to a regular conditioning practice carried on from the first day of practice to the last.

Our schedule consists of seven (7) games, all played on Thursdays, with the exception of the first game. Home games are played on the High School field at McCaskey at 3:30 P.M. Away games are played at the various teams fields or the High School of that city. Boys are transported by bus, and a meal provided after the game. We arrive home before eight o'clock in the evening. Thirty (30) boys are carried on the trips away from home.

Each boy is completely outfitted with the best equipment provided by the school board.

Practice and physical examinations begin on Monday of the third week in August at 9 A.M. at the school. Usually we practice every morning, beginning at 8:30 A.M. until school commences, and then after school until 5 or 5:30 P.M.; therefore, your son should be home soon after six in the evening. No practice Saturday, Sunday, or Labor Day.

School regulations require that every boy be examined at this time. It is very important for the boy to attend every practice especially those pre-school workouts. His chance of making the team depends on his being there.

Our discipline is very strong; this is necessary in every sport and school where success is to be gained. But please be assured that every boy will be treated fairly and be given every chance to make the team. Our fine success last season (we won every game) was due to this type of instruction, plus 100% cooperation on the part of a wonderful group of boys, and there is no reason why the coming season cannot reach the same heights.

Thanking you for your cooperation,

I remain,
Sincerely yours,
Samuel J. Thompson Sr.
Head Coach

REMINDER:

Physical at Reynolds, Monday, August 22nd, 9 A.M.

SUGGESTIONS:

Be in good physical shape by this date
Do a reasonable amount of running
Practice: *Sit-Ups*
Leg Lifts
Push Ups

REMEMBER: It is what you want to accomplish that you will accomplish.

A TEAM THAT WON'T BE BEATEN CAN'T BE BEATEN

A BOY THAT HAS DESIRE TO MAKE GOOD WILL MAKE A SUCCESS

A GOOD ATTITUDE SPELLS SUCCESS

See you,
Coach Thompson

Outline of Junior High Football Procedure for a Season

JOHN REYNOLDS JUNIOR HIGH, LANCASTER, PENNSYLVANIA

Prepared by: Head Coach Sam Thompson(16 years experience)

Permission cards to be signed by parents, and later signed by the examining doctor, are sent out in the spring. These are checked by the school nurse, and X-ray exam is noted thereon.

A letter to the parents is sent by the coach during the summer (sample enclosed). Also a letter to the boy, explaining the date of the physical exam, and a little of what is expected of him in pre-conditioning during the summer.

First Day

The Junior High School physicals are held at the school in the morning of the first day of practice; this is a Penna. P.I.A.A. rule. Full equipment is issued to each boy after the exam, and practice is scheduled for that afternoon (not in full equipment, that day).

Second Day

Due to hot weather at that time of the year, we schedule our practices in the mornings. On the field at 9 A.M.

9:00	Boys warm up with pass drills for a short time while coaches look for exceptional boys
9:15	Call squad together, and go over the following:
	Meaning of the game
	Discipline
	Training
	Attendance (a must)
	Promptness
	Scholastic achievement to be met
	Politeness in school
	Season schedule
	Treatment of equipment
	Treatment of injuries procedure
9:30	Line up and have warm up exercises
9:45	Line up in position lines, i.e., Centers, Guards, Tackles, Ends, Backs. Have wind sprints. (Look for speedy boys . . . lazy boys . . . indifferent boys)
10:10	Line coach take linemen and explain, demonstrate, and have boys go through stances. Backfield coach do the same with backs
10:30	Both coaches explain: OFFENSE—meaning DEFENSE—meaning (at this age, some do not know the difference)
11:00	Have a few wind sprints
	END OF SECOND DAY PRACTICE

Third Day

9:00	Warm-up . . . kickers begin to try out
9:15	Exercise (calisthenics, grass drills, agility drills)

9:30   In two lines ... Line and Backs go over stances ... Charging

9:50   Line ... with coach, practice easy blocks and charging– pulling

Backs ... with coach, Circle ... demonstrate and practice, holding and carrying the ball. Hand-off's—QB to backs. Pass drill—short passes

10:30   Entire squad for instruction on set up of OFFENSE. Explain each position, number of hole, etc.
WIND SPRINTS AND GO HOME

Fourth Day

9:00   Same time schedule. Warm-ups

9:15   Calisthenics, grass drills, agility drills

9:30   Review preceding day's activities briefly
Step up work with backs to methods of running with ball and avoiding being tackled. Such as: pivoting, cross over, stiff-arm, spin. Line—stances, charging, pulling, contact by shiving on each other

9:50   Begin defensive pass drills—one on one

10:15   Take last 45 minutes with entire team to go over offense again

A. Give two main plays (we usually begin with the OFF-TACKLE)
Walk through only with every candidate for back-field
Left and right side
End run the same way

B. Ask for questions, assign these two plays and assign two more for the next day. We find it easy for the beginner to learn plays, which are new to him, if we take each hole in the line and give them the play for that hole, and begin to alert them of the sequences that can be developed from same, such as the pitch-out off the end run

The delayed pass from the fake line plunge, etc. Do not do more than they can understand; this you will know by the experience or non-experience you are working with
End day's work with relays in place of wind sprints

Fifth Day

9:00	Warm-up free (on own initiative)
9:10	Exercise (calisthenics, grass drills, agility drills)
9:20	Talk to squad on progress ... begin to build up desire and enthusiasm
9:30	Divide backs and linemen

Line:
Using dummies, linemen begin blocking with an intent
Begin easy contact work in blocking
Backs:
Review ball handling
Fumble recovery drills
Pass drills
Work in backfield sets on handling ball for actual plays
Spend 15 minutes on blocking

10:00	Entire squad in two lines

Review all blocks in mass drill (same with tackling)
Shoulder—Left and Right
Angle—Left and Right

10:20	Divide squad into two teams and run through first four plays, against dummies. Assign two more plays to be studied for tomorrow
11:00	WIND SPRINTS AND GO HOME

(Could have kickers and other specialists out in the
P.M. and work with them for an hour)
You are now up to the beginning of the second week

Sixth Day

9:00	Free practice (15 minutes)
9:15	Exercise (calisthenics, grass drills, agility drills)
9:25	Talk to squad ... inquire as to blisters, check those absent, continue meaning of the game
9:30	Review:

Line: Go at blocking full ... One on One, Open field
one on one, circle drill
Backs: Fumble drill, blocking drills (same as Line),
pass drills
Run plays ... backs and centers only

10:00	Entire squad for blocking and tackling mass drills—two lines facing each other—Lanes

10:15	Entire squad in teams for signal drills
	We begin to stress the situation where each play will work
11:15	WIND SPRINTS AND GO HOME

Seventh Day

8:45	Free warm-ups
9:00	Exercise (calisthenics, grass drills and agility drills)
9:10	Two lines down under punts, touch receiver
9:30	Mass drills for blocking and tackling at half speed— Lanes, Circle, Groups
9:50	Signal drills and pass scrimmage
10:15	Signal drills for plays and one half speed scrimmage
11:15	Relays and go home

Eighth Day

9:00	Warm-up (calisthenics, grass drills, and agility drills)
9:10	Mass blocking and tackling drills—Groups: 2 on 1, 3 on 2, 1 on 1—Lanes (Two Lines interchanging)
9:20	We introduce a drill using four dummies
	Three linemen back of them to tackle, three linemen opposite side, to block for backs to run through any hole back wants to go. Very effective drill
9:40	End practice by:
	Going over punting formations offensive
	Run through at least a dozen kicks using all punters
	No opposing defense as yet

Ninth Day

9:00	Same preliminary work (warm-ups, calisthenics, agility and grass drills)
9:20	After exercise, have mass drill on blocking and tackling (15 minutes)
9:35	Using two squads begin to go over defensive work in units
	Run easy plays against different defenses
	Walk to full speed as they progress
10:15	Using remaining time set up kick off routine
	Show positions offensively and defensively
11:00	WIND SPRINTS AND GO HOME

Tenth Day

9:00	Warm up, exercise, and wind sprints
9:10	Down under punts
9:30	Review kick off
9:45	Hold a scrimmage for every candidate
11:10	Wind Sprints
11:15	Talk to squad, announce practice schedule for after school hours

A week before the first game we have a scrimmage with an outside school. Usually a Friday or Saturday. If scrimmage was held on Friday (tenth day), this practice session would be held on Saturday. The following practices are to correct mistakes brought out in the scrimmage. They will be integrated in the schedules of the next five days.

Warm-ups

Punting is polished

Kick-off practice [each evening afterwards]

Down under punts [every day]

Pass defense [stressed every day].

Movies shown of Senior High games of last year. Talk to squad to build up confidence and desire to make a good record this year. Remind squad of importance of studies. We stress attendance of our boys at Senior High school games.

After school starts, we are on the field at 4:00 P.M. and try to conclude the work by 5:30 each evening.

Monday

4:00	After two-day lay-offs (weekends), we review ball handling with backs, while charging and blocking is reviewed with line
4:15	Backs practice pass drills—offensively and defensively Line chicken fights and forms pass pocket
4:30	Mass blocking and tackling drill
5:00	Last 45 minutes, we have signal drill on dummies and full team scrimmage
5:45	WIND SPRINTS AND GO HOME

Tuesday

4:00	Report on field for free warm-up
4:10	Exercise . . . calisthenics, grass drills, agility drills

4:20	Mass blocking and tackling
4:30	Drills for linemen and backs (according to weakness as shown to date)
4:50	Down under punts ... 10 minutes Kick off drill ... 10 minutes
5:10	Review defenses and stress bread-and-butter plays
5:30	WIND SPRINTS AND GO HOME

Wednesday

4:00	Calisthenics (5 minutes) cover opponents weakness and strength
4:20	Drills with two squads—drilling on individual holes, slow speed to full speed. Work on each play until satisfied, both left and right
5:00	Pass scrimmage
5:20	WIND SPRINTS OR RELAYS

Thursday

GAME

Friday (Day after Game)

Regular Season Routine

NOTE: Seven game schedule and games are played in the afternoons, all games usually on Thursdays. Time: 3:30 P.M.

One game Saturday for city championship.

After season gets under way, Friday practice consists of varsity warm up and light signal drill. Thirty (30) minutes work with reserves—teach fundamentals. Monday and Tuesday review mistakes and go over drills—stressing blocking and tackling. Practice opponents defense.

4:00	Warm-up drills (agility-reaction)
4:10	Review mistakes of game, set mental attitude for next opponent Light signal drill and dismissal
4:40	Work with reserves on fundamentals—Scrimmage about 30 minutes

Monday

4:00	Agility and reaction drills
4:10	Remedial work based upon mistakes and weaknesses of Thursday's game. Stress blocking and tackling drills.

4:30	Review next opponent's strengths and weaknesses and strategy (plays plus defense) you have planned to use against them
5:00	Controlled scrimmage
5:30	Wind sprints and go home

Tuesday

4:00	Agility and reaction drills
4:10	Punt and kick-off drills
4:30	Pass offense and defense drills
4:45	Blocking drills (2 on 1, 5 on 3, 1 on 1)
5:00	Tackling drills
5:10	Review plays—Add new ones whenever needed
5:30	Wind sprints and go home

Wednesday

4:00	Agility and reaction drills
4:10	Review opponent and own strategy for game on Thursday
4:30	Drills (dummy) on kick-off blocking and punting . . . also cover punt coverage and going down under kick-off
4:45	Dummy pass coverage (offensive and defensive)
5:00	Review all plays to each side, extra point plays, goal line plays
5:30	Pep talk and sprints

SUMMARY

Midget football programs are blossoming all over the country but in a true sense the young football player actually gets his baptismal competition on the junior high school level. Competent coaches are assigned to teach the basic fundamentals along sane physical health standards. Facilities and equipment are provided to assure the best safeguards while the complete program receives the most stringent supervision. The practice plan is centered to the age and physical maturity of the participants eliminating as much pressure duress as possible. Simplicity and repetition are the keynotes of the practice schedule with the majority of the time allocated to teaching fundamentals either on an individual or mass scale. Patience, understanding and encouragement is demanded from the coaching staff. The amount of material to be taught is limited because of the physiological capacity of the boys. Practice, thus, is accelerated in accordance with progress being made. As veteran coach, Sam Thompson, so aptly summed it up, "We must start from scratch with these kids. Cripes! Some don't even know how to lace their shoes."

5

THE SMALL TO MEDIUM
HIGH SCHOOL SCHEDULE

Geared to Limited Staff

Any small or medium high-school practice program must be organized with the knowledge that its administration will be conducted by a limited one- or two-man coaching staff. Because the small school coach has twice the problem of his colleague in a larger school, it is imperative that he adopt a workable plan of practice action. Thus it is a good idea, whenever feasible, to schedule the opening game at least four weeks after the initial practice session. Without a junior high or jayvee feeder system there would be too many skills and fundamentals to be mastered by inexperienced boys. Even the experienced boys on a squad of this type should get the advantage of four weeks' preparation, since they will be called upon to shoulder the major burden of the demands of the team—quite often at more than one position.

Planning the Small School Practice

The small school coach seldom has too much free time during the day as he normally carries a full load of teaching, sometimes with a homeroom assignment as well. Therefore, it is advisable for him to prepare his practice schedule prior to the start of the football season. It will then take but a few minutes to check the schedule daily and make required revisions.

Since the majority of a small school squad will be composed

of beginners or boys of limited experience the apportionment of time is an important factor to consider. The intricacies of football teaching can tax one person's patience and energy drastically even with a well-planned practice schedule. The material to be presented to the boys must then be budgeted carefully to bring about the end results—namely, getting the squad ready for games.

To assure drawing up the best possible schedule, the coach should, first of all, do considerable thinking about the material which will be available for the coming season. He should make mental notes and list on paper the weaknesses of his boys and the fundamentals they need most such as speed, pulling, ball-handling, fakes, blocking, tackling, and timing. The good qualities of the squad should be recognized so that time could be allocated to those skills needing improvement. Offensive and defensive formations should be added to this list of basic fundamentals with the philosophy in mind that all boys on the squad are beginners. You start from scratch, then list coherently, step by step, all phases of the game to be taught to the individual boys with game readiness as the end result.

Plan Practice With Aid of Staff

Naturally, the small school coach, and definitely the medium size school coach, should consult any assistant or assistants making up the coaching staff and incorporate as many of their ideas as can be fitted into his own plans and strategy. There is a certain loyalty and family relationship in a two-man coaching staff, especially after several years' association, not usually found in a larger coaching staff.

Plan Must Keep Players Actively Engaged

The one-man coaching staff should plan his drills in such a way that all of his boys will be positively engaged in some activity even though he will be working with them separately. Thus, while he drills the linemen on pulling, cross-blocking, and charging, the backs will be actively engaged in ball handling, blocking dummies, and running plays. He must also plan his first week in such a manner that backs and linemen will be taught the same drills since in most cases he will have little, if any, ideas on definite positions for the individual members of the squad. Last season's fullback may be this fall's tackle and vice-versa. Other possible position changes may be necessary due to lack of depth, position needs, maturity and growth of players.

Plan Must Be Carried Out Almost Religiously

And finally, the allotment of time to each activity must be religiously followed. Quite often the one-man, and even two-man coaching staff, will feel that they are not accomplishing enough in the time designated. Inexperienced boys are not showing the progress the coach feels is required for improvement. He goes over the time limit, then he must either cut out other listed activities or increase the practice period, which results in listlessness, loss of learning transfer, and enthusiasm. If the practice schedule calls for two hours, stay within or near this time limit. Expose the boys to the work; the pieces will fit into the over-all endeavor. Remember that your rival coach is experiencing a similar dilemma.

Specialities and Off-Field Activities

Specialities such as place kicking, kick-offs, punting, passing, receiving, etc., are usually covered before the formal commencement of practice. Normally the boys are on the field earlier than the coach due to sundry pre-practice duties such as taping or equipment adjustments. Blackboard sessions can be held at the discretion of the coach while the football manual will provide other essential information. Quarterback strategy can be covered by the coach and his field generals at mutually convenient times. Often it is recommended to cover this important phase of the game with the whole squad since it is not unusual to find a senior tackle, guard, or center, calling both defensive and offensive signals due to their over-all playing experience. Often it is a wise policy to have two men check the offensive play before giving it to the offensive huddle.

The Small High School Pre-Season Practice Plan

The following three-week schedule of daily practice sessions is presented mainly for those coaches who find themselves in school systems without junior high schools, working unassisted or with one aide; and with squads numbering from 18 to 33 boys ranging in age from 13 to 18 years (some states extend limits to 19 and 20 years of age). This program was used at Cherrytree (Pa.) High School, enrollment 135; and Newport (Pa.), Joint High School, enrollment 245, by the author as a one-man coaching staff and later with one aide, Stanley P. Houser.

NOTE: Morning sessions should emphasize conditioning and the teaching of new skills and drills via dummy (simulated) conditions. Shorts are recommended as the dress uniform for morning sessions.

FIRST WEEK

Monday

Morning

9:00	Calisthenics (which includes grass drills, reaction and agility drills)
9:20	Wind sprints—by position, i.e., guards, tackles, centers, and ends, and all backs
9:35	Loose ball recovery (stationary and live)
9:45	Stances—by position
10:00	Charging from stances—short 5 to 8 yards, backs simulate receiving the ball (this will be emphasized in wind sprints hereafter)
10:10	Three man laterals up and down field (200 yards)
10:25	Orientation to two-man charger-blocker (C-B), blocking dummies, air aprons, and if available the seven-man sled
10:45	Introduce squad to the different types of popular offenses which may be encountered during season. Let them get visible pictures by lining them up in the different formations and explaining the strong and weak points of each
11:00	Goal post to goal post dash (220 yards)

Lunch

1:30–2:30	Blackboard session. Outline activities to squad that will be covered on field. This will economize time for the one-man coaching staff. Dressed in full gear onfield at 3:15
3:15	Calisthenics (grass, agility, and reaction drills)
3:30	Wind sprints—length of field and back (always by position)
3:40	One 220-yard dash
3:45	Ball recovery drill
3:55	Review line and backfield stances
4:00	Three-man laterals (length of field and back)
4:05	Fundamentals of passing and receiving. Explain fakes, throwing, catching, running after catch. Form passing lanes
4:30	Linemen on C-B, Backs on dummies . . . switch after 15 minutes. Cover crossbody blocks, shoulder blocks, head push, shiv, and tackling on C-B. Roll blocking, crab blocking (all-fours maintaining contact) and shoulder blocking on dummies
5:00	Finding punters and receivers
5:15	220-yard dash

Tuesday

Morning

9:00	Calisthenics (grass, agility, and reaction drills)
9:15	Wind sprints by position
9:25	One 220-yard dash
9:30	Recovery of loose ball
9:35	Review stances
9:40	Pulling and leading interference (all boys)
9:55	Three-man laterals
10:05	Fundamentals of passing and receiving
10:20	Punting, kick-off and place kicking drills to find the specialists
10:45	Fireman's carry
10:55	Two 220-yard dashes

Lunch

1:30–2:30	Blackboard Session
3:15	Calisthenics (grass, agility and reaction drills)
3:25	Wind sprints
3:30	One 100-yard dash
3:35	Recovery of loose ball
3:40	Tip drills
3:50	Pulling and leading interference
3:55	Review of stances and initial charge
4:00	Passing and receiving
4:15	Charger Blocker, dummies, sled
4:40	Shoulder to shoulder push
4:50	Ball handling drill ... handoffs from potential QB or direct snap backs from center
5:10	Wind sprints and dashes

Wednesday

Morning

9:00	Calisthenics (grass drills, agility, and reaction drills)
9:15	Wind sprints
9:25	Two 220-yard dashes
9:35	Huddle and offensive formations ... hole designation
9:55	Zig-zag running between spaced men, in rope course and rubber treadmill
10:10	Fireman's carry
10:20	Three-man laterals
10:25	Pulling drill
10:35	Ball handoff drill or direct snapback
10:45	Search for specialists ... punting, passing, kicking
11:00	Two 220-yard dashes and tire obstacle course

Lunch

1:30–2:30	Blackboard Session
3:15	Calisthenics (grass drills, agility and reaction drills)
3:30	Wind sprints (220 yards)
3:40	220-yard dash
3:45	Huddles, formations, basic plays ... dives or quick openers to give all boys feel of play and watch for backfield talent

4:10	Pulling drill
4:20	Zigzag drill
4:30	Demonstration and slow practice (live-moderate resistance) in the proper techniques of tackling
4:50	Demonstration and half speed in the techniques of blocking
5:05	Passing and receiving
5:15	Two 220-yard dashes
	Tire obstacle course

Thursday

Segregate Linemen and Backs.

Morning

9:00	Calisthenics
9:15	Wind sprints
9:25	Two 220-yard dashes
9:35	Backs punting and receiving . . . Linemen recovering punts
9:50	Linemen pulling drills . . . Backs zigzag-spinning drills
10:00	Passing and receiving drill
10:15	Fireman's carry drill
10:20	Kick-off with blocking responsibilities and coverage (up to the middle, right side, left side)
10:35	Huddles, formations, shifts, snake (for blocking simplicity) automatics, and bread-and-butter dive plays
11:00	Two 220-yard dashes
	Tire obstacle course

Lunch

1:30–2:30	Blackboard Session
3:15	Calisthenics (grass, agility and reaction drills)
3:30	Wind sprints
3:35	One 220-yard dash
3:40	Shoulder to shoulder drill
3:50	Linemen: Gauntlet
	Backs and Ends: Tip drill, intercepting drill
4:00	Linemen: Pulling drill on dummies
	Backs and Ends: Zigzag drill and one-handed receiving drill

4:10   Linemen: Drills on C-B or seven-man sled
Backs: Blocking on dummies
(Rotate personnel on C-B, sled and dummies)

4:40   Backs punting and receiving, linemen down under-coverage

5:00   Live kick-off drill

5:15   Two 220-yard dashes
Tire obstacle course

Friday

Morning

9:00   Calisthenics (grass, agility, reaction drills)

9:15   Wind sprints

9:25   Two 220-yard dashes

9:35   Offensive plays ... in addition to dive plays add power off-tackle plays to both sides, sweep plays and pitch-outs plus four bread-and-butter pass plays ... this will give you your basic offense ... henceforth add plays according to your offensive philosophy

10:10   Cover 4-man defenses and 5-3-2-1 defenses (a recent survey of Pennsylvania football revealed that over 90% of the schools use multiple defenses) pass coverage—man-for-man, zone, semi-zone

10:35   Backfield drills—gauntlet, diving into bags, zigzag
Linemen drills—Gauntlet (open hand resistance) pulling, pursuit drills

10:45   Kick-off review

10:55   Fireman's carry

11:00   Two 220-yard dashes
Tire obstacle course

Lunch

1:30–2:30   Blackboard Session

3:15   Calisthenics (grass, agility and reaction drills)

3:25   Wind sprints

3:30   One 220-yard dash

3:35   Shoulder to shoulder

3:40   *Linemen:* Defensive tactics (10 options *)—(1) sprinters charge; (2) shiver; (3) submarine; (4) over; (5) knife;

* *Athletic Journal* featured all ten via pictures in their April, May, and June 1960 issues.

(6) free leg; (7) split (arms and butt); (8) loop; (9) shoot the gap; (10) slant

Backfield: Ball handling, tip drill, zigzag, gauntlet, passing, reaction to passing

Ends: Steps; rushing, retreating, floating, one-handed drill, tip drill, hook, hook and go, change of pace, spot, speed (for the easy TD)

4:10	Whole squad: Offensive tactics—one-on-one; two-on-one; three-on-one; post; wedge; cross-blocking; hitting the linebackers; trapping
4:40	Blocking and tackling on C-B
4:55	One-on-one, two-on-one live scrimmage
5:15	Two 220-yard dashes
	Tire obstacle course

Saturday

One practice only (preferably in the Morning)

9:00	Calisthenics (grass, agility and reaction drill)
9:15	Wind sprints
9:20	One 220-yard dash
9:25	[General review of week's work] . . . ball recovery drill
9:30	Stances, huddle, shifts, holes
9:35	Three-man laterals
9:40	Fireman's carry
9:45	Shoulder to shoulder push
9:50	Linemen: Pulling and gauntlet
	Backs: Zigzag and gauntlet
	Ends: Steps, pass lanes, with fakes
10:00	Line: Pursuit drills
	Backs: Rotation drills
10:10	Line: Review 10 defensive tactics
	Backs: Pass defense
10:15	Line: Cover offensive line blocks (post, double team, etc.)
	Backs: Passing, receiving, pass defense drills
	Ends: same as backs
10:30	Line: Charger-blocker, sled
	Backs: Stiff arm techniques—dive into bags on goal line
10:45	Two-on-one scrimmage
11:00	Punting, receiving, coverage . . . live

11:25   Five-man scrimmage (ball carrier, blocker, center, end man and backer-up—backs can fill in with ends as end men, tackles, guards, centers, and fullbacks as backer-ups)

11:30   Two 220-yard dashes

SECOND WEEK

Monday

Morning

9:00   Calisthenics (grass, agility and reaction drills)

9:15   Wind sprints (440 yards—by position—220 yards at a time)

9:25   Two 220-yard dashes

9:35   Review 4-4-2-1 defenses with stunting variations *
Also 5-3-2-1 conservative and with stunting variations
Add 6-2-2-1 with variations, i.e., tight, loose, conservative (Pass)
Cover 6-3-2—with slants and loops
Pass defense for each

10:10   Run offensive plays against a mixture of these defenses rotating personnel. Add three new pass plays, 2 trap plays, draw, counter play, statue of liberty, reverse play and running pass play

11:00   Two 220-yard dashes
Tire obstacle course

Lunch

1:30–2:30   Blackboard Session

3:15   Calisthenics, etc.

3:25   Wind sprints (220 yards)

3:30   One 220-yard dash

3:35   Linemen: Work on defensive tactics
Backs: Run offensive plays (running)
Ends: Practice slashing, steps, covering outside, dropping for pass defense or rotation

3:55   Linemen: Work on offensive tactics
Backs: Give 4 basic goal-line plays and let them practice

---

* For variety of defenses the author recommends *Simplified Multiple Defense,* Prentice-Hall, Inc. Englewood Cliffs, N. J.

4:15   Linemen: on C-B and sled
          Backs: on dummies and air aprons

4:30   Pass scrimmage: offensive linemen forming pocket; secondary defensing the pass

4:45   Punt scrimmage: protecting the punter and coverage

4:55   P.A.T. scrimmage: protecting the kicker

5:05   Live scrimmage for 10 minutes to give boys a feel of the game

5:15   Two 220-yard dashes
          Tire obstacle course

Tuesday

Morning

9:00   Calisthenics, etc.

9:10   Wind sprints . . . 440 yards

9:20   Two 220-yard dashes

9:30   Introduce 7-man defensive line (7-diamond, 7-Umbrella)
          Review 4-, 5-, 6-man lines

9:50   Add P.A.T. running and pass plays; punt running and pass plays; spread plays (if you have them in your repertory) NOTE: the survey of Pennsylvania Football by the author showed conclusively that over the past three years the best winning records were achieved by schools with 100 or more offensive plays

10:15   Run through your goal line plays against a seven, eight, nine and eleven man defenses

10:40   Triangle style, coach in middle review all offensive plays. (Coach calls out play . . . teams run through them one by one under Coach's scrutiny)

11:00   Two 220-yard dashes
          Tire obstacle course

Lunch

1:30–2:30   Blackboard Session

NOTE: Since so many schools play their first game after three weeks of pre-season practice the recent trend has been to schedule at least two pre-season practice games with non-scheduled opponents. Alteration of this schedule would hinge on dates these games would be played. The day before would correspond to any practice night prior

to a game the succeeding day. The order of activities would be light
with warm-ups, review of plays, defenses and orientation on opponent. The day after the scrimmage would also be light with a general critique of the scrimmage.

3:15	Calisthenics, etc.
3:25	Cover 8-man defenses . . . conservative 8-3 and gap-8
	Cover 9-man defense . . . for inside 2 yard line
	Cover goal line defenses
3:50	Circle blocking drill
4:05	Controlled scrimmage (Coach calls plays and defenses)
5:10	Review mistakes . . . deliver little pep talk
	Run a 100-yard dash

Wednesday

NOTE: Many coaches make a practice of calling off the morning
session to restore player enthusiasm, relieve the daily monotony of
two-a-day sessions, and give the one- or two-man coaching staffs a
breather. Through Tuesday practice has run a 15 session grind. A
morning rest is to be recommended. For the coach who feels he must
practice the following morning schedule is outlined.

9:00	Calisthenics, etc.
9:15	Wind sprints
9:20	Dashes by position—25, 50, 75, 100 yards
9:30	Orientation on scrimmage opponent or first rival
9:45	Linemen: Pulling drill
	Backs and Ends: Passing
9:55	Line: Dummy scrimmage on protecting passer and cross-blocking on air aprons
	Backs and Ends: Pass offense and defense (Man-to-man, zone, or semi-zone)
10:10	Review offensive plays against multiple defenses
10:30	Two 220-yard dashes . . . tire obstacle course

Lunch

1:30–2:30	Blackboard Session
3:15	Calisthenics, etc.
3:25	Wind sprints
3:30	One 220-yard dash
3:35	Fireman's carry, shoulder to shoulder drill

3:45   Tackling drill. Two lines inside the five yard stripes, backs standing, leading lineman lies on his back head pointing to back, feet away. Both are five yards apart. Coach yells "go" upon which signal he flips the ball high or away but within reach of back who gets it and attempts to get by lineman who surges to his feet, turns, and attempts to tackle back.

4:00   Blocking drill (similar to tackling drill except that lines are mixed and both are standing with backs to each other five yards apart. On signal one side attempts to crossbody or shoulder block the other man. Men interchange)

4:15   Circle tackling drill

4:30   Circle blocking drill

5:00   Pursuit drill (scrimmage)

5:15   Two 200-yard dashes ... tire obstacle course

Thursday

NOTE: An inter-school scrimmage is recommended. Perhaps the scrimmage could be scheduled for Wednesday. Regardless, the practice schedule should be elastic to permit any change. If a scrimmage is scheduled, the morning session should be cancelled; and a chalk session should be the procedure. If a scrimmage game is not scheduled, then the morning schedule would call for an over-all review of skills, offense and defense, and strategy.

The afternoon would be either:

Inter-school Scrimmage ⎫ Controlled, Coaches on field correct-
Intra-Squad Scrimmage ⎬ ing mistakes, etc.

Friday

Morning

9:00   Calisthenics, etc.

9:15   Wind sprints

9:20   One 220-yard dash

9:25   Critique of scrimmage ... cover good points, praise, then go over mistakes; run through offensive or defensive weaknesses

10:00   Review all offensive plays, add any new ones you feel is needed to make your offense more varied. Run plays in triangle style

11:00   Two 220-yard dashes ... tire obstacle course

Lunch

1:30–2:30   Blackboard Session

3:15   Calisthenics, etc.

3:25   Wind sprints

3:30   One 220-yard dash

3:35   *Remedial Day.* Outline your afternoon practice schedule immediately after the morning session. The scrimmage should have brought out various weaknesses as a team or individually. You can also base your judgment on what you have observed during the two weeks of two-a-day sessions. If blocking is weak, schedule blocking for at least 30 minutes on the dummies, machine or live. Go over punting, kicking-off, P.A.T., passing (all phases) and tackling

5:15   Two 220-yard dashes . . . tire obstacle course

Saturday

NOTE: While many coaches may disagree due to the short lapse of time (one day only) a scrimmage with another school or the same opponent of Thursday would be in order. It could be arranged for Monday, but the week preceding the first game should be used for timing, polishing up, tapering off, and getting ready for the first opponent. Frankly speaking, high school boys don't bruise easily and have strong recuperative physical powers. They have boundless energy. Consider also the fact that Thursday's scrimmage was controlled and included all of the playing personnel, thus spelling each boy to a degree.

Saturday: Morning or afternoon—one session only. Inter-School scrimmage or full-scale intra-squad scrimmage.

THIRD WEEK

School begins—sessions are cut to one-a-day. Time limit may also vary from 1 hour, 1½ hours, or 2 hours. The following schedule is suggested. You can alter it to fit your own needs.

Monday

(Some schools start practice at 3:30; others during the noon recess so jointure students can ride buses home)

4:00   Warm-ups (agility and reaction drills . . . players should take calisthenics as they hit the field on an individual basis)

4:10   Review of Saturday's scrimmage and correction of mistakes

4:25   Go over multiple defense rules. The majority of schools according to the Pennsylvania Survey use more than one defense in a game. The range is from 2 to 9 with the average at 3 per game. Have your defensive units face different offensive formations

4:40   Stress and run through the basic defense to be employed against first opponent. If old scouting reports are available, allow the defense to deploy against some of the running plays and passes. Cite alternative defenses to be used against this first opponent

5:00   T-formation one-on-one blocking by line. Backs circle blocking and circle tackling

5:10   Punting, receiving, and tackling drill

5:20   Kick-off scrimmage with return options and defensive coverage

5:30   Punting and P.A.T. scrimmage

5:40   Offensive and defensive pass scrimmage

5:50   Eight-man tackling drill (offensive center and two guards or tackles, blocker and ball carrier ... defensive lineman, end man and linebacker)

6:00   880-yard run (in 220-yard dashes with rest intervals)

Tuesday

4:00   Warm-ups

4:10   Linemen: Pulling drill, review defensive tactics
        Backs: Zigzag, gauntlet, bucking bags on goal-line

4:20   Line on C-B or sled
        Backs and Ends: Pass offense and defense

4:40   Sideline drill ... 3 blockers and ball carrier against 3 tacklers spaced 15 yards apart. Tacklers 10 yards inside the sidelines coming across field

5:00   Line: one-on-one, 2 on 1, 3 on 1, 5 on 2
        Backs: C-B, dummies, circle blocking drill

5:20   (Scrimmage, if game is on Friday) Assuming game is on Saturday ... offensive plays (bread-and-butter)

5:40   Defensive scrimmage ... defensive unit against reserves, etc. employing plays that opponent runs

6:00   880-yard run

Wednesday

4:00	Warm-ups
4:10	Line: Pulling drills and gauntlet
	Backs: Ball handling drills (tip, loose ball, zigzag)
4:20	Review first opponent, strength, weakness, offense (favorite plays, trick formations, etc.) and defenses that might be encountered
4:35	Line: on C-B, sled and dummies (all blocks and tackling)
	Backs: alternate with line on dummies, C-B, etc.
4:55	Review offensive plays (triangle style)
5:20	Review kick-offs
5:30	Offensive scrimmage
6:00	880-yard run

Thursday

4:00	Warm-ups
4:10	Backs: Drills and offensive plays
	Line: Pulling and review defensive tactics
4:30	All alternating on C-B, sled and dummies
4:50	Review punting and coverage, kick-offs, P.A.T.
	Linemen executing necessary blocks or releasing
5:05	Review goal line defenses
5:15	One-on-one, 2 on 1 drills (linemen)
	Backs: circle tackle drills
5:25	Review goal line offensive plays
5:35	Pass offense and defense (dummy scrimmage—moderate resistance)
5:45	Run plays up and down field briskly
6:00	440-yard run

Friday

4:00	Warm-ups
4:10	Review opponent again and cover own strategy, i.e., offense and defense plus alternatives
4:30	Run goal line plays against goal line defenses
4:40	Run through all pass plays, P.A.T. plays, punt plays, spread plays, and trick plays
5:00	Review remainder of plays in triangle
	Pep Talk
6:00	One fast dash
	Skull Session (30 minutes)

Saturday

GAME

If game is played at close of fourth week of practice, follow about the same schedule during fourth week as run during third week with some possible alterations by way of remedial work.

The weekly practice schedule during the season will be covered in Chapter 11 while off-field activities, such as blackboard sessions and scouting, will be treated in Chapter 10. Chapter 9 will deal with the training of the specialists.

SUMMARY

Much in the manner of the junior high school program the small high school coach must gear his program to a limited coaching staff which in many cases could be himself, and to a limited group of players many of whom are totally inexperienced. Practice must be planned on the assumption that the whole squad is inexperienced which means the teaching from scratch of all skills that will serve as new experiences for the beginner and a review for the veteran player. Players must be taught all drills regardless of position played previously since the coach of a small squad will have to switch many positions to plug possible weaknesses. Oftentimes players from squads of this nature are called upon to play more than one position. Because of such limitations the coach must plan his program in such a way that classroom duties, lack of assistance and possible limiting facilities will not hinder his program to any noticeable degree. Players must be kept positively busy at all times whether supervised or not. Time is at a premium so it must be economically apportioned. Thus, it is recommended that the small high school coach draw up the best possible pre-season practice schedule well in advance of the start of formal practice. It may also be recommended that it would be more feasible from a preparedness standpoint to schedule the first game four weeks from the opening of practice because of the many skills and game technicalities that must be learned quite often by inexperienced boys who in many cases are in the majority of squad personnel.

Coach	1	2	3
CAMPUS	CAMP	CAMP	CAMPUS
W. ARRV.	M	M	M - CLASS START
T	T	T	T
F	W	W	W
ST.	T	T	T
SUN (T)	F	F	F
	S	S	S - FIRST GAME
		SUN (T)	

6

THE LARGE HIGH SCHOOL
PRACTICE PROGRAM

Large High School Demands Greater Organization

While time may be the chief problem of the limited staff in spreading themselves among the different positions demanding attention, the problem facing the head coach of a large high school is primarily one of organization. The larger coaching staff and greater number of player personnel involved, reaching all the way into the junior high schools, poses a major task of organization and supervision.

It is not unusual for a coach in a large high school to open practice with a hundred or more boys. These boys must be given every opportunity to exhibit their talents because, often as not, the star of tomorrow may be in the ranks of the total group. One year of maturity in most boys can be as different as day or night. The same boy that showed little promise a year ago on the junior high or jayvee team may turn out to be this year's ace player. Thus the coaching staff must know their functions well, and activities must be apportioned in such a way that every boy will receive individual attention and feel that he is given every opportunity to make the squad. Often it seems to be a waste of a coach's time with certain individuals who do not possess the reflexes and natural skills required by the game. Yet, if these boys are overlooked, they can influence other boys, parents, and townspeople with their gripes—the most common being that the coach has already picked his team, thereby inferring partiality. The result can be low morale and a drop in personnel turning out for the squad in the ensuing years. Many large high school teams have faced this dilemma. Squad morale, discipline, cooperation and mastery are results of good practice organization.

Discretion a Keynote

Delegation of functions to a large coaching staff must be done with extreme discretion. Since more individual supervision is possible time must be apportioned according to the experience, need, and mastery shown by each position. Quite often coaches feel that they must work their separate charges religiously and actively for the entire practice period whether it be one-and-one-half hours or two hours. They fail to evaluate the mental and physical condition of the boys thereby giving credence to an oft-quoted expression, "They left their game on the practice field."

In organizing the parctice sessions objectives should be established and made clear to the entire staff. Practice should be terminated when the coach or his assistants feel the objectives have been accomplished. This infers that a two hour practice session could be called at the end of an hour and a half. Dragging it on to consume the other half hour will not produce any fruitful results and may lead to indifference and loss of morale. The coach and his staff must be constantly aware of the temper and emotions of the squad. Know when to work and when to stop. In a large high school this is important. In the opinion of many coaches an hour and a half of dynamic activity will produce more positive results than two hours of habitual practice. This is especially true and recommended once pre-season practice is finished. With veteran material an hour of practice can be sufficient. I enjoyed a 11-0 slate in 1953 and never practiced more than an hour. It got to a point where my squad begged for more practice time, because they were never satiated in 60 minutes. I, however, could feel the pulse of the squad and knew that an hour met all of our needs. This was evidenced by averaging 39 points per game and allowing only four touchdowns for the entire season.

SAMPLING OF A LARGE HIGH SCHOOL PROGRAM

Pre-Season Varsity Football Practice (Three Weeks)

HIGHLANDS HIGH SCHOOL, FORT THOMAS, KENTUCKY
Homer Rice, Head Coach and Owen Hauck, Head Line Coach

Our practice organization reflects our entire approach to coaching football. We have learned to believe in a much repeated adage, "You play the game exactly like you practice." A team becomes disciplined, well-coached, spirited and crowd-appealing if these are the goals you have every day of your pre-season practice. Nothing can be left to chance in modern day football. Every possible contingency must be provided for in your planning, or some autumn week-end will be the saddest day of your life.

We have tried to base our football at Highlands on the following five basic points: *morale, dedication, movement, speed, and desire.* Those five words sum up our philosophy and approach to the game. They cannot be given any priority of importance. Leave any one of them out of your mental picture of football and you cannot build championship teams. If they become a part of your coaching staff's make-up, then they will permeate the atmosphere of your locker room and practice field, and stamp the players of your teams with the axiom, "well-coached."

The first three weeks of football practice must be preceded by careful planning. It is necessary for the coach to have a good summer conditioning program for his players to follow, or they will show up out of shape and unable to stand the hard grind of preparing for the opening game. If you have to spend the first three weeks just conditioning your squad, then it is certainly going to be a long fall with victories few and far between. We try to overcome this by providing a work-sheet for each player to follow throughout the summer vacation. Twice during the summer, short conferences are held with the players to check on their general progress so we may aid them in solving any problems that have arisen. We send form letters to any of our squad that may be out of town for the summer, in order to keep in contact with them.

Orientation Week

One week before practice officially begins, we have a general orientation week. This is possible for us, as the state of Kentucky does not place a restriction on the starting time of practice. Every effort is made during this week to eliminate the usual mix-ups that sometimes impair the smooth running of the first week of practice. Generally, the following four things are accomplished during this week:

1. Medical examinations and insurance coverage are handled. _MANDATED condition tests_
2. Parent's Night is held. _- PICTURE DAY_
3. Equipment issued usually by order of class. _& Fitted properly_
4. Final staff meetings in anticipation of opening practice sessions.

5. ORIENTATION TO VARIED MISCELLANY

The staff will meet in conference each day of this first week to prepare for the first session on Monday morning and to get a general understanding of the type of football we will be coaching. This attention to detail seems to stir renewed interest on the part of the staff and instills a sense of confidence into the players, their parents, and our fans, that we mean business and again hope to put forth a winning football team.

Staff Organization

The football staff at Highlands consists of four coaches and a full-time trainer. This necessitates that we double-up on some coaching assignments. Though the reader will find this practice organization plan (see accompanying charts) designed for four coaches, it can readily be adapted to a two-man staff. In reality our Head Coach handles offense planning, offensive and defensive backs, and over-all organization. The Head Line Coach handles defensive planning and offensive and defensive linemen. They are assisted in early season practice by the two junior varsity coaches until their squad reports, which is one week prior to the beginning of school. Generally, the varsity squads consist of forty members. Though no one is ever cut from football unless for disciplinary reasons.

Staff Meetings

Staff meetings are the heart of football practice organization. Here is the place where the staff members can thrash out the myriad problems that will face them from day to day. The Head Coach should preside as chairman of these meetings, but he should be careful to allow every member of his staff an opportunity to offer ideas and make suggestions. Considerable latitude should be allowed each assistant in organizing the phases of practice in his area of responsibility. However, the Head Coach must bear the responsibility for the final format of the practice schedule.

Our staff meetings are held as soon after the morning and afternoon practices are over as possible. We find this a most convenient time, since the problems that have arisen during practice are fresh in our minds. We give a considerable part of this time over to the evaluation of player personnel as we are trying to find our best boys during the first three weeks. It is sometimes necessary to move players from one position to another to provide a better balanced squad. The two staff meetings also provide us with a chance to add needed drills, or rearrange our allotted practice times. It is rarely necessary to have late evening meetings using this method. However, it may be necessary to meet during the weekends to view films and make alterations in the coming week's program.

Movies

A period is arranged in our practice day for the showing of last year's game movies or training films we have available. The first full scale game type scrimmage we have is filmed, and we study this closely with the players. This is usually done right after lunch. Generally this is done by positions under the supervision of one of the coaches. The films of previous years can be used in the training of offensive quarterbacks and defensive signal-callers by going over the strategy used in those games and pointing out the strong and weak points of the opponent's defense, and in reverse order on our own game procedures.

Penalty Period

In order to issue one hundred per cent knowledge of assignments we have inserted a penalty period in our practice sessions. This is held after the movie period. The whole squad generally witnesses the penalty period. Anyone who has missed questions on assignment tests must report for the penalty period on the practice field. One of the coaches will handle this period. The boys have to begin running circle sprints in one direction and then the coach blows a whistle, which signals him to return in the opposite direction. This continues for a stated time in relation to how many questions he missed. Needless to say, performing before the whole squad in such a manner lends itself to bringing about perfect papers in the future.

Planning the Practice Schedule

The first three weeks of our practice has long before been worked out by our coaching staff. A general practice plan (Chart 1) has been thoroughly worked out to include every

Chart 1

DAILY TIME SCHEDULE

Morning

7:45– 8:15	Staff Meeting (Coaches dress ready to go) tapers, wrappers, report to trainer
8:15– 8:30	General Squad Meeting (Head Coach)
	Lord's Prayer
	Announcements
	Offensive play for the day (one play a day)
	(squad reports to meeting in shorts—must be taped or wrapped before 8:15)
8:30– 9:00	Group Meetings (teach new play for the day)
	Offensive Line Coach takes linemen
	Offensive Backfield Coach takes backs

Chart 1 (*continued*)

DAILY TIME SCHEDULE

Morning

9:00– 9:15	Squad puts pads on for the morning practice
9:15– 9:20	Squad Meeting before reporting to field (Head Coach briefs squad on morning practice procedure)
9:20	Squad and Coaches report to practice field ready for warm ups
9:20–11:00	Morning Practice (1 hour 40 minutes)
11:00–11:45	Shower, check injuries, check equipment
11:45–12:30	Staff Meeting

Afternoon

2:00–3:00	Film Showing and Penalty Period
2:30–3:00	Trainer reports in for taping, wrapping
3:00–3:15	Squad General Meeting (Head Line Coach in charge)
	Announcements
	Defense for today
	(squad reports to meeting in shorts—must be taped or wrapped before 3:00)
3:15–3:45	Group Meetings
	Defensive Line Coach takes linemen
	Defensive Backfield Coach takes backs
3:45–4:00	Squad puts pads on for afternoon practice
4:00–4:05	Squad assembles for practice procedure assignments
4:05	Squad and Coaches report to field for afternoon practice session
4:05–5:30	Afternoon Practice session
5:30–6:15	Shower, check injuries, check equipment
6:15–7:00	Staff Meeting

aspect of the football day for three weeks. Then a detailed morning (Chart 2) and afternoon practice (Chart 3) have been charted. A definite assignment of coaching responsibilities has been made (Chart 4). We have a check-off list printed on a large piece of cardboard hanging in our office, which we refer to as

Chart 2

MORNING PRACTICE SCHEDULE (OFFENSE)

9:20– 9:25	Warm up period (Squad together)
9:25– 9:30	Buddy Drill (Four Groups)
9:30– 9:35	QB warm up passing drills
	Backs: Pass protection drill
	Centers, Guards, Tackles, Ends: Gap Blocking Drill
9:35– 9:40	Center: QB exchange drill
	Backs, Guards, Tackles, Ends: Fumble Drill (2 minutes)
	Backs: Inside-out blocking drill
	Guards, Tackles, and Ends: Downfield blocking drill
9:40– 9:50	Backs: Play drill
	Centers and Guards: Quick Trap Drill, Double Team Drill
	Tackles and Ends: Double Team Drill and Hook and Trap Drill
9:50–10:00	Backs and Ends: Pass Drill
	Centers, Guards, and Tackles: Wedge Blocking and Pass Protection
10:00–10:05	Special Drill Period. (Coach selects one such as The Hand-off Challenge Drill, Hamburger, Double Hamburger)
10:05–10:10	3-Team Signal Drill
10:10–10:40	Offensive Team Drill
	3-Down Zone
	4-Down Zone
	Scoring Special Zone
10:40–10:50	Specialty Period
	Punt Returns
	Kick Off Returns
10:50	20 Yard Sprints
	First Week—20
	Second Week—30
	Third Week—40
	40 Yard Dash on Time
11:00	Shower

Chart 3

AFTERNOON PRACTICE SCHEDULE (DEFENSE)

4:05–4:15	Kicking Drill for Punters, K. O., and receivers.
	Individual linemen position instruction (Middle Guard, Linebackers, Tackles, Ends)
	Sled Extension Drills (While coach works with one position, others work on sled)
4:15–4:20	Defensive Buddy Drill (four groups)
4:20–4:30	Backs, Linebackers: Pass Defensive Drills
	Middle Guard, Tackles, Ends: Pursuit Drills
4:30–4:40	Back, Ends: Pass Defensive Drills
	MG, LB, T: Stunt Techniques
4:40–4:50	Backs, Ends, LB: Defensive coverages
	MG, T: Eagle Techniques
4:50–5:20	Team Defense
	Goal Line Defense (Inside 10-Yard Line—include extra point and field goal attempt)
	4-Down
	3-Down
5:20–5:30	Specialty Period
	Tight Punt
	Spread Punt
	Kick Off
	Safety
5:30	Shower

time goes on, to make sure we are not omitting any phase of our preparation for the coming season. It has been omitted from this chapter by the authors, because we felt every coach would prepare his own in relation to what type of football he teaches. We feel, also, that a printed calendar of each day's activities, prominently displayed in color on the office wall, serves as a reminder to the staff of the over-all pre-season planning. It also serves to keep the coaching staff conscious of the passing of precious time and the approach of the opening game.

Chart 4

COACHES PRACTICE SCHEDULE ASSIGNMENT _ A. M.

	AIRNS	DULL	BARAN	CURL
TIME (A.M.)	HEAD COACH OFF QB-DB	HEAD LINE DEF G|C TNT	ASS'T BACKS RB-LB	ASS'T LINE KICK TIES
9:20– 9:25	Lead Warm-Ups	Check Warm-Ups	Check Warm-Ups	Check Warm-Ups
TAKE-OFF 9:25– 9:30 SHOULDER SKILLS	Buddy Drill Group 1 (Backs)	Buddy Drill Group 1 (Line)	Buddy Drill Group 2 (Backs)	Buddy Drill Group 2 (Line)
9:30– 9:35	QB Warm-Up Passing	Centers, Guards Tackles, End (Gap Blocking Drill)	Backs—Pass Protection	KICK SKILLS Help Head Line Coach
9:35– 9:40	Center-QB Exchange Drill	Group 1 (Line) Fumble Drill, Downfield Blocking Drill	Backs—Fumble Drills, Inside-Out Blocking Drill	Group 2 (Line) Fumble Drill Downfield Blocking Drill
9:40– 9:50	Backs—Play Drill ON HOSE	Center, Guards—Trap, Double Team Drill	Help Head Coach	Tackles—Ends Double Team, Hook and Tap Drill
9:50–10:00	Backs, Ends— Pass Drills	Centers, Guards, Tackles— Wedge Blocking and Pass Protection	Help Head Coach	Help Head Line Coach
10:00–10:05	Lead Special Drill	Check Special Drill	Check Special Drill	Check Special Drill
10:05–10:10	3-Team Signal Drill—check all teams	Check Team 1	Check Team 2	Check Team 3
10:10–10:40	Offensive Team, Check team and backfield assign.	Offensive Team, Check Team and Line Assign.	Defensive Backs	Defensive Line

Chart 4 (continued)

COACHES PRACTICE SCHEDULE ASSIGNMENT

TIME (A.M.)	HEAD COACH	HEAD LINE	ASS'T BACKS	ASS'T LINE
10:40–10:50	*Specialty Period* Check Backfield Punt and Kick Off Return Assign.	Check Linemen Assignments for Punt and Kick Off Return	Offensive team Punting and Kick Off	Offensive Team Punting and Kick Off
10:50	*Sprints* Check Running	Start Odd	Start Even	Check Running
40-Yard Dash	Time Group 1 (Backs)	Time Group 1 (Line)	Time Group 2 (Backs)	Time Group 2 (Line)
Shower	Preparation for Staff Meeting	Check Equipment	Check Equipment	Check Equipment

Chart 5

COACHES PRACTICE SCHEDULE ASSIGNMENTS (AFTERNOON)

TIME (P.M.)	HEAD COACH	HEAD LINE	ASS'T BACKS	ASS'T LINE
4:05–4:15	Kicking Drill (Check Punters, Placekickers)	Individual Defensive Line Keys (Select a position)	Kicking Drill (Check Receivers)	Sled Drills for Linemen not in Line Key Drill
4:15–4:20	Buddy Drill Group 1 (Backs)	Buddy Drill Group 1 (Line)	Buddy Drill Group 2 (Backs)	Buddy Drill Group 2 (Line)
4:20–4:30	Pass Defense (Halfbacks and Safetys)	Pursuit Drills (MG, Tackles, and Ends)	Pass Defense (Line backers)	Help Head Line Coach
4:30–4:40	Pass Defense (Backs and Ends)	Stunt Techniques (MG, LB's, and Tackles)	Help Head Coach	Help Head Line Coach

Chart 5 *(continued)*

COACHES PRACTICE SCHEDULE ASSIGNMENTS (AFTERNOON)

TIME (P.M.)	HEAD COACH	HEAD LINE	ASS'T BACKS	ASS'T LINE
4:40–4:50	Defensive Coverage (Backs, Ends, and LB)	Eagle Techniques (MG and Tackles)	Help Head Coach	Help Head Line Coach
5:20–5:30	Specialty Period Check Punter and Kick Off Team	Punting and Kick Off Team	Receiving Team	Receiving Team
Shower	Make Preparation for Staff Meeting	Check Equipment	Check Equipment	Check Equipment
4:50–5:20	Team Defense Check Secondary	Team Defense Check Line	Team Defense Offensive Team	Team Defense Offensive Team

Training Rules

The first squad meeting on Monday is devoted to the outlining of our general procedure to the squad and setting up our training rules. This is done by the head coach, and he usually makes a brief talk about squad morale and points to the goals we hope to achieve. We have found that a positive approach to what we are attempting to do has elicited tremendous response from our football teams. We want the boys to believe that they can be champions, and that the starting point is his mental attitude.

Our training rules are brief and have been the following for eight years:

1. No smoking.
2. No drinking of alcoholic beverages or carbonated water soft drinks (one Coke is permitted after a Varsity Game).
3. No profane language on or off the field.
4. Off the streets—8:30 P.M.

5. Lights out—9:00 P.M.
6. Week-ends (Friday and Saturday—11:00 P.M.).
7. No cars permitted unless absolutely necessary (walk or ride a bike).
8. Go the church of your choice every Sunday.
9. Perfect attendance to practice.
10. Practice sportmanship on and off the field. There is *no* substitute for character.

The head coach then outlines our specifics as far as football practice is concerned.

1. Wear all of your equipment during practice. Never remove headgears.
2. Never kneel or sit down, stay on your feet.
3. No water allowed during practice or game.
4. Sprint everywhere on the practice field. Don't walk or jog; football is based on movement.
5. Take 100% care of your equipment and facilities (we have the best—let's keep it that way).
6. Report every Monday with clean knit wear.
7. Clean and polish shoes. Be sure to dry properly after being wet.
8. Remember we must be 100% in our knowledge of assignments (even 99% might be failure on Friday night).
9. Never be late. Remember the kickoff is 8:15 not 8:16.
10. Pride is our watchword.

Daily Routine Schedule

The general daily schedule is then given to the squad. We urge them to follow our advice as to eating time and diet (suggested training diets are handed out in mimeographed form) as closely as possible. Generally, we suggest the following:

1. Lights on 6:00 A.M.
2. Breakfast—6:30 A.M.
3. Lunch—12:00 P.M. (at home)
4. Dinner—6:30 P.M.

5. Off streets—8:30 P.M.
6. Ovaltine—8:45 P.M. (a good relaxer that started as a joke and has become a tradition for the team and coaching staff)
7. Lights out—9:00 P.M.

Squad Meeting Procedures

The early morning meeting, after the first day, then becomes a teaching period. We open all our meetings with one of the squad members leading us in the Lord's Prayer. This has become a tradition at Highlands. For years it has been our pre-game ritual and our players ask us to start every meeting of our pre-season practice with a prayer. It has lifted the general outlook of our squad and puts us in a serious frame of mind for the work ahead. After the prayer, the head coach outlines the play we plan to add to our offense. We have found that to add a play a day helps us to master the techniques thoroughly. We pass out mimeographed sheets to the players and then project the same play on a screen by means of viewgraph projector. The sheets are designed so the player can take notes and then enter them in the proper place in his notebook. We then split the squad into backs and linemen for a more detailed discussion of their assignments under the guidance of the backfield and line coach. These morning meetings continue throughout the first three weeks. We hold them to forty-five minutes or less because the players tend to lose interest in a longer session.

All our practices begin with a squad assembly in the varsity locker room. The head coach briefs the squad on the practice procedure and clears up any questions at this time. We seldom interrupt our practice schedule for lengthy explanations by the coaching staff, and we want the players to clear up any questions on assignments, etc., in this meeting. Our squad understands that we are going to be on the practice field for just one hour and forty minutes, but that it is to be a period of concentrated activity. The Senior manager is entrusted with the job of moving us from period to period by blowing a whistle. We give him a schedule of our practice and tell him to keep track of the time so we will move from drill to drill. Every coach has a tendency to stay too long on some particular phase of the game, thus, failing to follow his scheduled practice plan. By delegating this responsibility to the manager you will keep your practice moving from period to period on time.

In preparing this chapter the authors felt it might be more meaningful to carry through the exact plan of one day's morning and afternoon practice. Thereby we could insert drills and training techniques just as we use them in definitely allotted time sequences of our schedule. Of course there is nothing sacred in the arrangement of the time periods. This is only one of many available avenues of procedure. However, it has been kind to us and we hope it will provide a starting point for beginning coaches, and will stimulate thought for more experienced mentors. Various drills are explained in some detail as they come in our time periods.

MORNING PRACTICE SCHEDULE (CHART 2)

9:20–9:25   Warm-up

The players are lined-up facing the head coach who leads the calisthenics. They are grouped in a semi-circle by position. We do the following exercises by hand signals to develop concentration.

1. Fundamental Football Position
2. Quick-steps (Wave Drills)
3. Wind Mill
4. Knee Stretch
5. Crotch Stretch
6. Sit-Ups (grab-cleats-pull)
7. Grass-Drill (hit dirt on signal)

9:25–9:30   Buddy Drill (Four Groups)

Throughout our pre-season practice, and in fact during the entire campaign, our warm-ups are followed by a period of buddy drills. We pair our boys up by position and divide them into four groups.

Diagram 1

The buddy drills are designed to teach the fundamentals of our fire-out block (Shoulder block). We have the following objectives in this drill:

1. Teach Stance (Later to check only)
2. Teach Fire-Out Technique (We find it is best to teach this block in the beginning by reverse progression in the following order.
   a. Lifting Action (Put the boy in the position in which you want him after contact. Later in our practice session we will drop this teaching phase.)
   b. Full Extension (Having offensive man fall out on catcher's knee from a fundamental position.)
   c. Fire-Out. (From stance fire out on snap count putting the two above techniques together. Roll out of stance, extension, pop, lifting action. Keep head up (look for treetops) and past the hip of opponent. Feet must move if you do this.)
   d. Challenge Drill. (Offensive man is placed in good blocking position and on command, the defensive man attempts to throw him off. Whistle stops drill.)

9:30–9:35   Q.B. Warm-up Passing Drill

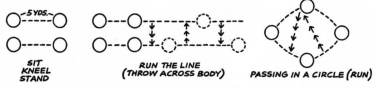

Diagram 2

The quarterbacks work on passing from the following positions: (1) sitting, (2) outline from both knees, (3) one knee, (4) run the line, (5) pass in circle.

Backs—Pass Protection

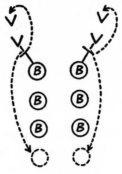

Diagram 3

Gap Blocking Drill (Centers—Guards—Tackles—Ends)

Diagram 4

This drill provides us an opportunity to work on what can be a bothersome problem, lineman charging the gaps. Here we attempt to teach:

1. Step with on-side (near) foot
2. Aim for shoulder at opponent's knee
3. Follow through with all-fours crab block (This drill employed both right and left)

9:35–9:40   *A. B. Exchange Drill* (Center)

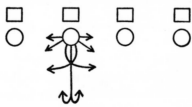

Diagram 5

Stress:

1. Commanding Voice (Snap Count)
2. Head and Shoulder Looks
3. Open and reverse turns
4. 20, 40, 60, 80 Series
5. Drop back, Roll out, Sprint out passes

Circle Fumble Drill (2 minutes)— (Backs, Guards, Tackles, Ends)

Inside Out Blocking Drill (Backs)

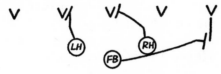

Diagram 6

This drill is designed to teach the proper approach on position blocks for our backs. The technique is the same as the fire-out block, only the backs have a running start.

The main coaching point is to have the boy take the proper inside out approach. All the backs alternate being defensive men. This drill is run full tilt but defensive men offer little resistance in order to facilitate teaching.

Downfield Blocking Drill (Guards—Tackles—Ends)

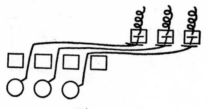

Diagram 7

We run this drill usually against stand-up dummies but at times with live bait. All linemen release inside dummies or defensive men.

The main coaching points:

1. Take correct approach to get in front of ball carrier.
2. Run to man and then try to drive head and shoulders through him.
3. At last moment bring forearm across the body and throw hips into opponent, attempting to double him up.
4. Stress rolling three times.

9:40–9:50   Play Drill (Backs)

Offensive Backfield Coach will teach execution of the new play added in the morning meeting.

Quick Trap Drill and Double Team Drill

The Assistant Line Coach will stress proper techniques in trapping and double teaming against odd and even defenses.

Double Team Drill–Hook and Trap Drill (Tackles and Ends)

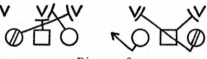

Diagram 8

The Head Line Coach checks and teaches the double team post-drive principle to the tackle and end and teaches them to hook and trap.

Diagram 9

9:50–10:00   Pass Drill (Backs and Ends)

The various pass routes are run with the boys working in two groups. The number one quarterback is used with the number one receivers to get them accustomed to working together.

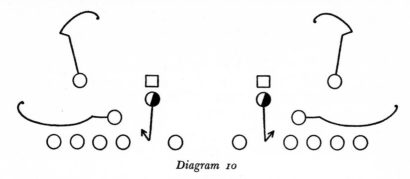

Diagram 10

Wedge Blocking and Pass Protection
(Centers, Guards, and Tackles)

The Line Coaches teach the wedge block that plays such an important part in our offensive football. They instruct the outside lineman to work his inside shoulder in under the armpit of the man to his inside toward the apex. They must stay high and drive hard. They cannot go down at any cost. After a short drill on the wedge, the pass protection techniques and rules are employed.

10:00–10:05   Special Drill Period
(For reaction, agility, and morale)

Coach selects one of the following special drills for each morning practice: Hand-off Challenge Drill, Hamburger Drill, Double Hamburger Drill.

The hand-off challenge drill is a multi-purpose drill which we feel covers many important aspects of ball carrying for backs.

1. Center–Q. B. Exchange
2. Stance–Take off–starting count
3. Hand-off–Look through hole
4. Ball carrier must break through two air dummies held by two linemen that push them together just as the back is reaching the line of scrimmage.
5. The ball carrier must get his feet up and eyes open to hustle over the standing dummies lying about three yards apart.

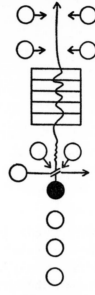

Diagram 11

6. Then he must run a gauntlet of six linemen that try to make them fumble.
7. We try to get this done in 4.0 for 25 yards as a challenge.

The Hamburger Drill is the best one in football to find your aggressive players.

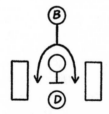

Diagram 12

1. Place an offensive and defensive man opposite each other between two large standing dummies.
2. Place a ball carrier five yards behind the offensive man.
3. The offensive man tries out on his own.

4. The back drives straight up and cuts the opposite way the defensive man is being taken.

5. The defensive man employs all his techniques to shed the blocker and make a driving tackle.

6. We feel this drill helps us to find football players and at the same time teaches the basic fundamentals of tackling, blocking and running with the ball.

Our double hamburger is a "killer" drill designed to develop rough, tough, aggressive linemen, who really like contact. It also aids in finding backs that will drive in there and get the necessary yardage under the toughest conditions.

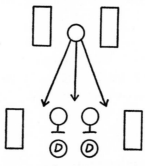

Diagram 13

1. Place two offensive men opposite two defensive men between two stand up dummies.

2. Have a back lined up five yards deep behind the offensive men.

3. One coach stands behind the defense and signals the offensive men which way to block. The back tries to cut behind or go between the blocks.

4. This drill stimulates live game contact better than any drill we have seen.

10:05–10:10   *Three Team Signal Drill*

Break from huddle
Run Dive right and left
F. B. up the middle
Q. B. sneak

Main Coaching Points:

1. Huddle break
2. Basic line spacing
3. Lining up on the ball
4. Take off on signal count
5. Return to huddle

10:10–10:40   Team Period (Stressing offense)

3 Down Zone—from our goal line to opponent's 40
4 Down Zone—from opponent's 40 to the 10-yard line
Special Zone—inside opponent's 10-yard line

We spend ten minutes to each zone. The plays best suited for each situation are used. Our quarterbacks are encouraged to run plays always with field position in mind. This sets up a pattern to our offense early in the year.

10:40–10:50   Speciality Period

Punt Return (5 minutes)
Kick-off return (5 minutes)

The punt return is the only phase of our defensive planning we have in our morning practice. This is necessary because our kicking drills are set up in the afternoon during our first three weeks.

10:50   20-Yard Sprints

1. Players are lined up by position.
2. Coach starts them on regular sound.
3. We insist on full effort or we add one additional sprint. (No jogging)
4. Players immediately lined up for return and the process is repeated in the opposite direction.
5. We build up to forty sprints on Friday.

6. The sprints have become a tradition to our squads, and they feel this is the deciding factor in our out-lasting many opponents in the final quarter of a game.

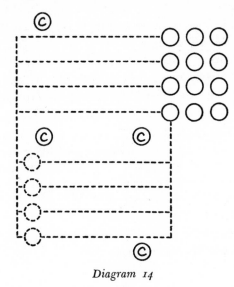

Diagram 14

10:55   40 Yards on Time

1. Players are divided in four groups and timed by a coach.
2. We start the watch when the player's hand leaves the ground.
3. A manager with a clipboard records the times. They are later posted on the squad bulletin board.
4. We strive for every starter to run a 5.2 40.
5. It has been amazing the improvement every boy makes as the season progresses.

AFTERNOON PRACTICE SCHEDULE (CHART 3)

The afternoon squad meeting is identical with the morning procedure except the emphasis is now on defense. However, the meeting is usually preceded by a meeting with the defensive signal callers and the head line coach who handles the over-all team defense. At this time, the head coach has a conference on offensive strategy with the quarterbacks. One defense is presented to the squad by the head line coach. The defense is passed out in mimeographed form and projected on the screen by means of the view-graph. After a general discussion of the defense, the squad is divided into two groups for specific instructions on techniques and alignment. Usually we break down the defense into the forcing and containing units. The head coach takes safeties and cornermen; the line coach, the linemen and linebackers.

A brief squad assembly is held for the purpose of outlining our practice for the afternoon after the squad has suited up. Generally both of our practice sessions are held in full equipment. On very hot days we may hold the afternoon practice in shorts, or if suited out, we will shorten our practice to one hour. We then assemble on the field and follow our time schedule as rigidly as the morning work-out.

4:05–4:15   *Kicking Drill for Punters, Receivers, K. O.,*
and Receivers

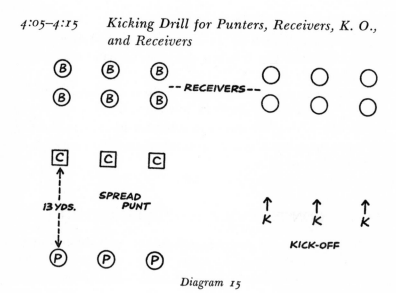

Diagram 15

Linemen—Crowther Drills

1. Six points—HIT—RECOIL— (3 times) right to left
2. Four points—HIT—RECOIL—(3 times) right to left
3. Three points—HIT—LIFT—SPRINT—5 yds, tackle dummy

Individual Linemen position instruction (Head Line Coach works with Linebackers, Ends, Middle guards on given days while the rest of the linemen go through their defensive drills on the sled.)

4:15–4:20   *Buddy Drill* (Four Groups)

Our linemen use the Ricochet Drill for warm-up purposes in the afternoon. This drill aids in developing the following fundamental techniques:

1. Defensive Stance
2. Charge
3. Forearm Lift (Right and Left Arm)
4. Quick Reaction

One offensive lineman will fire out. The defensive man meets the charge with forearm, gets leverage, and then quickly recoils to defensive stance. The opposite man fires out, and the process is repeated.

The backs will pair off and work on form tackling and then across the bow (side) tackling.

From time to time we will insert other basic defensive drills as we feel a need for them. It also varies the routine of daily drills.

The following drills might be used.

1. Bull in the Ring
2. Monkey Roll (agility)
3. One-on-One Drill (linemen)
4. Three-on-One Drill
5. Defensive Challenge Drill

4:20–4:30   *Pass Defense Drills* (Backs and Linebackers)

**BACK PEDAL AND
CHANGING DIRECTION**   **INTERCEPTION
DRILL**   **TAP
DRILL**

Diagram 16

The back pedal and changing direction drill serves several important purposes. The player starts back pedaling on a signal from the coach and then changes direction on a subsequent signal. After the coach has him change direction several times he will throw the ball in such a way as to have the player have to really take-off to intercept it. This last phase of the drill teaches the defensive back to go for the ball when it is thrown.

The interception drill is used to develop the ability to catch the ball coming toward a man on the run. The coach will have them come straight ahead and go right and left.

In the tip drill the coach throws the ball high to the first man running directly at him. After the man catches the ball he will tip it to the second man who tries to keep about five yards behind him.

Playing the Zone

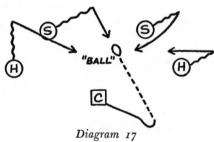

Diagram 17

Each member of the containing unit is taught to revolve to his zone on the signal of the coach. They will react to drop-back

and roll-out actions. The coach will then throw the ball, checking that all backs on the "ball." At times linebackers are added
in this drill.

One on One Pursuit Drills (Middle Guard—Tackles—Ends)
    5 Minutes

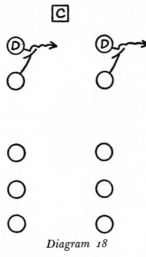

Diagram 18

Two men are placed on defense. Two offensive men opposite
them fire out and attempt to block the man right or left. The
defensive men deliver a blow and work laterally attempting to
shed the blocker. Later a ball carrier is added to increase competition.

Team Pursuit Drill (5 Minutes)

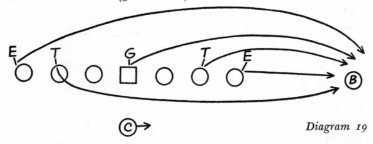

Diagram 19

The offensive team fires out without sound. The defensive
team delivers a blow and then looks to the coach who signals

pursuit right, left or pass rush. The forcing unit follow their correct pursuit angles to two players placed right and left. They all must tag the player. This adds enthusiasm and competition to the drill.

The following points are stressed:

1. Stance—Charge
2. Deliver a blow
3. Locate ball
4. Pursue—Right and left
5. Rush passer
6. Check draw
7. Check counter

4:30–4:40   *Pass Defensive Drills* (Backs and Ends)

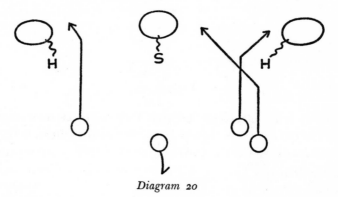

Diagram 20

Various pass routes are run by the ends. The three deep men are drilled to stop the home run pass and to come up and search the receivers. We want them to play through the receiver.

Stunt Techniques (Middle Guards—Linebackers—Tackles)

The defensive line coach drills on the various stunts from the basic Oklahoma defense. The crossfire, tackle X and other stunts are employed. This is usually done with little opposition so the defensive men can master fundamentals and assignments.

Every possible offensive set is reviewed in this period. The defense is taught how to cover flankers, wing, split ends, lone-

4:40–4:50   *Defensive Coverages* (Backs—Ends—Linebackers)

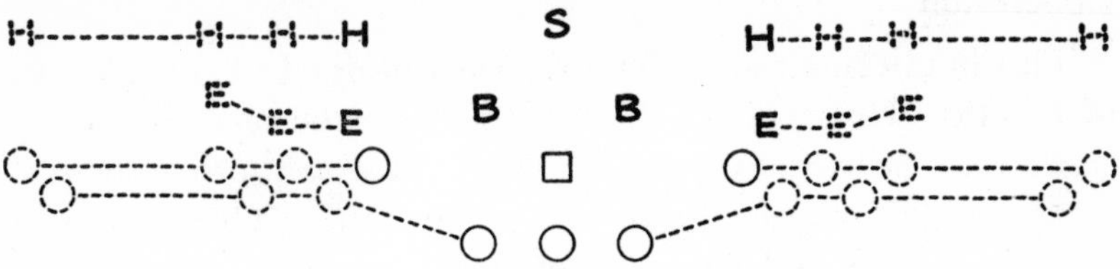

Diagram 21

some end, motion, double wing, etc. All the various types of pass patterns are run. Often this will be live for the secondary with full-steam tackling.

The following points are stressed:

1. Defensive secondary calls out offensive set.
2. Move quickly to proper rotation.
3. Three deep men never let any one get behind them.
4. Go for the ball when it is thrown.
5. React to interception. Lead ball carrier.

Eagle Techniques (Middle Guard and Tackles)

All the Keys are taught and reviewed for tackles. Middle Guard learns to check draw-screen pass—shovel pass. He is instructed on his part in covering the hook zones.

4:50–5:20   *Team Defense*

Goal Line Defense—Inside our own 10-yard line (10 minutes)

4-Down Zone—Inside our own 40-yard line (10 minutes)

3-Down Zone Beyond our own 40-yard line (10 minutes)

5:20–5:30   *Speciality Period*

Tight Punt (Inside 5-yard line)

Spread Punt

Kick Off

Safety (Once a week)

5:30   *Shower*

Conclusion

This has been a rather detailed study of our first three weeks of practice. However, modern football has become extremely complex. Therefore, it must be approached as thoroughly as a general would engage in an important battle. The difference between success and failure is often the attention you give to small details. If there is any secret to winning teams, it is the willingness of the coach to teach the sound fundamentals of the game.

The first three weeks are the crucial ones in preparing for the coming season. It is sad to hear a coach telling about his decision to return to the teaching of blocking and tackling after a 40-0 defeat. This should have been his first consideration, not a second thought. To find your way on a journey you must have a map. Even the early explorers of this country followed rivers and buffalo trails. A practice schedule, check-off list, coach's assignment sheet and practice calendar are your maps to a successful journey through the fall campaign.

SECOND WEEK—PRACTICE SCHEDULE

JOHNSTOWN HIGH SCHOOL
At Football Camp

Sunday

P.M.	No practice.	Squad meeting 7 P.M. to 9 P.M. Check notebooks. Go over First Week's progress
	9:30	Lights out for players
	9 to 10:30	Coaches meeting

Monday

A.M.	7:00	Breakfast
	7:20– 8:20	Rest
	8:20– 9:00	Taping
	9:00– 9:15	Get dressed for practice
	9:15– 9:30	Meeting
	9:30– 9:45	Loosening Up Drills (Alternate personnel, centers and quarterbacks)
		1. Ends with Center A and Q'B A. Pass Cuts

2. Guards and Tackles—with Center B and Q'B B on cadence, stance, and starts

3. Rest of Centers and Q'Bs—cadence and snap

4. Backs—Pocket drills for handoffs

9:45–10:00   Calisthenics

10:00–10:15   Backs—2-man sled drills (offense)

Line —7-man sled drills (offense)

10:15–10:30   Backs—Offensive drills (Select what needs emphasis and devote time accordingly)

1. Push-off drills
2. Shake-off drills
3. Tires drill
4. Down the board on handoff
5. Runner and blocker drill
6. Lower the boom drill
7. Improvised drills as needed

10:15–10:30   Linemen—Offensive drills (Select as needed)

1. Groups of two—cross blocking
2. Cross-field technique
3. Cross-shoulder technique
4. Double-team technique
5. Inside-out lift
6. Down field drill

10:30–10:45   Backs—Steps, techniques, unit drill on plays

Linemen—With Q'B #4. Full line techniques

10:45–11:30   Group A vs. Group D. Dummy scrimmage

Coaches Hart and Mahalic

Group A Offense

Coaches Fuchs, Statnik, and Zakula

Group D Defense (5-4 Straight)

Group B vs. Group C. Dummy scrimmage

Coaches Matsko and Slobovien

Group B Offense

Monday

A.M.   Coaches Kocerka and Svitchen

                                      Group C Defense (5-4 Straight)

11:30–11:40   Sprints

12:15 P.M.   Lunch

12:20– 1:45   Rest

1:45– 2:30   Q'B Meeting with Coaches Hart and
                   Kocerka

2:30– 2:45   Get dressed for practice

2:45– 3:00   Loosening Up

                   Jog—Players run three quarter-miles

                   Run and spin backwards.

                   Calisthenics (players at their own choice)

3:00– 3:15   Backs

                   1. Coming in on the ball

                   2. Tip drill

                   3. Reaction drill on pass defense

                   4. Approach and tackle drill

                   5. Forearm on blocker fight to ball car-
                      rier drill

                   Line

                   Sleds—defensive reaction drills

3:15– 3:45   Backs—Pass Defense

                   1. One on one

                   2. Two on one (zone)

                   3. Switch drill

                   4. Spot drill

                   5. Interception blocks and wall set-up

                   Ends—Rushing passer ten minutes, then
                         join line

                   Line—Defensive work. Reaction, spin
                        outs, pursuit, etc.

3:45– 5:00   Group work

                   Defense—70 per cent, Groups A and B

                   Offense—30 per cent, Groups C and D

5:00– 5:15   Specialties. *Everyone* stays out

8:00– 9:00   Squad meeting

9:00–10:30   Coaches meeting

Tuesday

                   —and rest of week, meal times and lights out the same as
                   Monday. Practices are preceded by meeting and held as

indicated for Monday. We go in early at times from practice as a reward for progress.

The first 15 minutes of each practice session is devoted to loosening up, with varied assignments which are posted or assigned at the meeting prior to practice.

Calisthenics depends upon our practice. We like to take calisthenics every morning from 9:45 to 10:00 A.M. In the afternoon we usually have loosening up exercises that do not warrant calisthenics afterwards.

After Calisthenics:

A.M.	10:00–10:15	Backs.	Live blocking—form technique
		Line.	One on one—form technique
	10:15–10:30	Backs.	Offensive drills (Select what's needed)
		Line.	Offensive drills (Select what's needed)
	10:30–10:45	Backs.	Interior plays and fakes into Group D linemen who converge on the Offensive back
		Line.	Offensive reaction drills
	10:45–11:30	Same as Monday schedule	
	11:30–11:40	Sprinting backwards	
P.M.	1:45– 2:00	Q'B meeting	
	2:00– 2:30	Ends and Backs meet on pass patterns	
	3:00– 3:15	Backs.	Defensive reaction drills
		Line.	Defensive reaction drills
	3:15– 4:00	Defensive work in units	
	4:00– 5:00	Full group Defensive work emphasized	
	5:00– 5:15	Specialties.	70 per cent Offense
			30 per cent Defense

Wednesday

A.M. Same as Tuesday with slight variation determined from coaches meeting

P.M. No practice. Unit meetings with players and coaches

Evening—full scale scrimmage, running game:

> Group A vs. Group C
> 7:00–8:15
> Group B vs. Group D
> 8:30–9:45

Thursday

A.M.   Unit work on offensive mistakes and weaknesses of preceding evening's scrimmage—for one full hour

Full group offense dummy—one hour

Q'Bs passing at tire target—20 minutes after practice

P.M.   Q'Bs, Ends, and Backs meet on pass patterns

3:00– 4:00   Backs and Ends, against full defensive backfield, work on techniques for pass patterns, screens, and draws

Line works on pass protection, screens, and draw blocking

4:00– 5:00   Full group work covering preceding hour

Friday

A.M.   10:00–10:30   Defensive drills and techniques

10:30–11:00   Unit defense drills

11:00–11:30   Full group defensive scrimmage

11:30–11:40   Pursuit sprints

P.M.   3:00– 3:30   Offensive drills and techniques

3:30– 3:45   Unit defense drills

3:45– 5:00   Group work (50 per cent Offense, 50 per cent Defense)

7:00– 8:30   Meeting—the kicking game and coverage

Saturday

A.M.   In sweat clothes or shorts, Group work—dummy

P.M.   Scrimmage game

Evening. Players off; no meeting

SUMMARY

The practice schedules included in Chapter 8 are examples of the type and content to be found in the larger high schools. They are well organized and the objectives clearly stated. The large high school program can be closely compared to the major college plan of practice. More player personnel and a larger staff is in evidence which demands almost the ultimate in organization and supervision. The contents of the practice plan must be arranged for expediency in coverage and the staff well oriented in their duties and responsibilities. Delegation of authority must be made with confidence and discretion. Every participant must be made to feel that he was afforded every opportunity to make the squad or the result may breed dissension and create a morale problem. The Highlands High School, Fort Thomas (Kentucky) and Johnstown (Pennsylvania) High School pre-season practice schedules featured in this chapter are completely pre-planned, and stress the importance of thorough planning. The first three weeks are crucial. The practice schedule, check-off list, coach's assignment sheet and practice calendar are essential in setting up the football journey through the fall campaign.

7

THE SMALL COLLEGE
PRACTICE PLAN

Small College Problems and Limitations

The small college coach found among the liberal arts and
teachers colleges has coaching problems akin to the small high
school coach. He is limited in staff, facilities, time, and by
teaching load. The general trend to amateurism by a majority
of the small colleges throughout the country has mandated
more teaching on the part of the coach and his limited staff.
The schools offering athletic scholarships normally take the
cream of the high school talent thereby leaving the immature,
underweight, or inexperienced boy for the small college coach
to develop. This demands much more time to be spent on teaching fundamentals; time that quite often is not readily available.

A. Staff

It is not unusual but rather the rule to find two men handling
a small college squad. The head coach may be either the line or
backfield coach with another aide to take the group not handled
by the head coach. Sometimes a freshman coach is provided, but
in most cases a local ex-athlete is hired to handle the team during the football season. Most small colleges have abolished the
freshman rule and allow participation by these first-year men.

B. Player Personnel

The player personnel can range from a squad of 33 to 100.
The small liberal arts college normally has a squad averaging

in the thirties while most colleges offering physical education curriculums and the numerous teachers colleges may have a turnout of 50 to 100 players. Selecting a playing squad from the latter categories with a limited staff poses a major problem. In addition, the majority of the colleges listed above do not offer scholarship inducements which limits the experience of the turnout. Since star athletes are not recruited there is more incentive for students with limited experience to turn out for the squad. It all adds up to the basic teaching methods where the head coach must organize his practice program under the assumption that his squad knows little, if any, football. Fundamentals must be taught and emphasized in greater detail and length.

C. Recruiting in the Small College

Perhaps a statement in the preceding paragraph may be misinterpreted when it was stated that star athletes are not recruited by the small colleges. This is erroneous in the sense that small college coaches do recruit but without scholarship inducements few can successfully attract a star athlete with the promise of a good education and a possible campus job that may earn the boy two or three hundred dollars a year. In the small liberal arts college such a job is of small significance in meeting yearly costs ranging from $1,500 to $2,200. Teachers colleges have an advantage because of financial aid from the state; thus a campus job looms larger in meeting low costs at the latter institutions since over-all expenses may range from $600 to $1000 yearly.

D. Limitations, Curtailed Program Has Eased Pressure on Small College Coach

In view of such limitations the small college coach must fall back on salesmanship and better motivating philosophies. He must organize in such a way that as much work as possible will be covered in the time available; and this latter condition may be as little as an hour daily with late class plus laboratory interference. In many cases pre-season practice is not endorsed by the college administration or it may be limited to one week. Add to these restrictions unsympathetic faculty members and you can easily visualize the immensity of the small college mentor's coaching problem. His only consolation in most instances is the easing of that ever constant pressure to win. In the majority of the small colleges not supporting athletic scholarships coaches have tenure, i.e., their job is not dependent upon the won-lost record. This produces a healthy situation since it allows the coach to be more human with his associates and players. As head coach, Woody Sponangle, of Franklin and Marshall College, Lancaster, Pennsylvania, clearly stated it after two years of a non-scholarship program, "I am enjoying coaching for the first time in years. I go out and have fun with those kids now, and it is surprising how much we accomplish in this pressureless experience." Under an athletic scholarship program F & M once dominated small college football. Since it dropped this program schools of similar status have been scheduled and with its new pressureless philosophy the college is still showing a winning ledger.

The Millersville State College Program

Millersville State College, a teacher-training institution, has been selected as the program indicative of most small colleges throughout the country. Here the staff faces the many problems and limitations found in a majority of similar small institutions of learning. From the standpoint of staff perhaps I am more fortunate than most colleagues in that I do have a line coach and a backfield coach. My freshman team (those who do not make the varsity squad) is tutored by two coaches recruited from the local high school which does not sponsor football. Until recently pre-season practice was not feasible. Last year we had two weeks of it. This year we will again have two weeks, beginning September first. Once these two weeks are completed, regular practice will begin at 4:30 P.M. and end at precisely 5:30 P.M. (to comply with dining hall regulations). Late classes, especially from the industrial arts department and student teaching, keep a number of players from practice two and three times weekly. Once daylight saving time ends our practices rarely go beyond 40 minutes. These are not exaggerations but facts. The administration is very sympathetic but football is treated like any other extra-curricular activity. It is secondary to the primary purpose of the college; namely, turning out the best teachers possible for the Commonwealth of Pennsylvania. It is a part of the college over-all development of the student and receives no special concessions. The staff is asked to do the best possible job within the limitations.

Practice Program Has Shown Positive Results

Our entrance requirements are very strict and admission is dependent upon several personal, intellectual, and scholastic factors. Entrance examinations (college board) are required of all students with minimum scores in the 450 to 500 range. Our 33 wins 33 losses and 1 tie over the last eight years may appear inferior at first glance, but when viewed from the standpoint of the above limitations the understanding coach will quickly agree the record is commendable. Our schedule includes some of the best small colleges in the East such as West Chester, Lock Haven, Bloomsburg, Trenton, Randolph-Macon, and others. Under the existing conditions we have had five winning seasons out of the last eight years. These facts are not being stated to invoke your sympathy or to make the Millersville program appear as an unhealthy situation, but rather to qualify the practice program and its organization as one that can insure results. The fact that our opponents and other small colleges have the same limitations decrees that the best possible plan of available time be utilized.

Program Based on Simplicity and Personnel

The program itself is predicated upon simplicity and its graduated development. It can be adaptable to any high school, because it is based upon the assumption that the squad is highly inexperienced; since we do get many boys without benefit of high school participation or boys who were reserves and saw very little action. We do have varsity performers but mostly from the smaller high schools. Lately our squad has been supplemented by transfer students from the major colleges. These boys must sit out a year under the NCAA transfer rule. Recruiting pays off with about 30 boys yearly after a complete coverage of the state contacting over 600 coaches by mail and an equal number of boys. These boys exhibit the above qualifications with perhaps four or five qualifying as blue chip boys for our brand of football. Thus we greet a squad of about 80 boys at first practice call and end the season with about 55. Our mortality rate is high from year to year. Without the binding obligations of a scholarship we usually end up with about five or six seniors out of the 35 freshmen we recruit. This is highly indicative of other institutions in the scholarship-lacking category.

Pre-Season Program Emphasizes Fundamentals and Acceleration

Such conditions then mandate a practice schedule based upon the barest fundamentals with accelerated development over a minimum period of days where economy of time is at a premium. Time prohibits new teaching to any degree once the season starts. We must teach and cover all phases of the game during the pre-season practice or our program will be amiss once classes begin. We start slow and move fast.

Organization of the Practice Program

The morning sessions are conducted mostly in shorts with heavy work in the afternoon. Since we play our games on Saturday afternoons we practice during identical hours to get the boys acclimated to the heat. Assistant coaches have the prerogative to use full equipment for the morning sessions after the first week. Each practice session is limited to an average of two hours. The third week's program is plotted for two hour sessions—although we only have a one-hour maximum at Millersville—for the majority of schools.

It can also be noticed how we integrate the many factors of the game such as conditioning drills, game drills, game mechanics, game skills, and framework fundamentals (the offensive, defensive and kicking game).

In administering the practice program each coach is briefed on his particular functions prior to practice. He lists on his clip board the activities he will direct individually. As head coach

I have the complete master plan for the session and go from
one group to another as an observer, advisor, or consultant. I
keep close check on the time element and blow my whistle
when a change from one activity to another must be made.
When periods for combined work are reached I call the squad
together and take over.

Millersville State Teachers College Pre-Season Football Practice Schedule

First Week—Orientation and Conditioning

MONDAY

8:00 A.M.   Coaches meeting

9:00 A.M.–11:00 A.M.   Dressed on field

15 Minutes—Calisthenics and grass drills (Conditioning)

5 Minutes—Bag and fire drill (Conditioning)

15 Minutes—Wind sprints— (a) straight dash, (b) rolls, (c) turn-
arounds (Conditioning)

5 Minutes—Ball recovery (Game drill)

15 Minutes—Stances, huddles, formations, hole numbering,
automatics (Game mechanics)

10 Minutes—Linemen pulling drill—Backs zig-zag drill (Game
drill)

10 Minutes—3-men lateral drill (Conditioning and game drill)

5 Minutes—Fireman's carry drill (Conditioning)

20 Minutes—Orientation to charger-blocker (Game skills)
Techniques in cross-body blocking, shoulder
blocking, shiving, tackling, and neck push drill

20 Minutes—Introduction of plays. Blocking rules explained—
timing emphasized; also mechanics (Framework
fundamentals)

Finish: 220-yard dash

12:00   Lunch

12:45   Coaches meeting

2:00–3:00   Skull session

3:30–5:30   Afternoon practice period

MONDAY

   10 Minutes—Calisthenics and grass drills

   10 Minutes—Bag and tire drill

   10 Minutes—Wind sprints (3 varieties)

    5 Minutes—Dashes (short—25 to 50 yards) and Speed drill

   10 Minutes—Review stances
             Backfield drills—Forward, sideways, counter
               (Game skills)
             Linemen pulling and charging drill (5 men)
               (Game skill)

   10 Minutes—Linemen snaking out of huddle to line of scrim-
             mage, assuming pre-snap stance, snap stance,
             charge on signal (Game mechanics)
             Backfield—Hand-off drill

   20 Minutes—Linemen on charger-blocker—Backs on dummies
             (Both groups exchange after ten minutes) (Game
             mechanics)

   20 Minutes—Introduce Five Man Defenses—53, 56, 57, 58.
             (Framework fundamentals)
             Explain Pass Defense: Zone, Semi-Zone, Man to
             Man

    5 Minutes—Shoulder to shoulder (Conditioning)

   15 Minutes—Review morning plays, add new ones

   Finish: 220-yard dash

   7:00 P.M.   Skull session to review day's work. Only 20 Min-
   7:20   utes

TUESDAY

   8:00 A.M.   Coaches meeting
   9:00 A.M.–11:00 A.M.   Two hour session. Squad on field ready to
             go at 9:00 A.M.

   15 Minutes—Calisthenics and grass drills

    5 Minutes—Bags and tire drills

   15 Minutes—Wind sprints (3 types)

    5 Minutes—Dashes (100 yards per dash)

10 Minutes—Linemen: 5-man pulling drill (Game mechanics)
     Backs: Practicing hand-offs, ball control, proper
        use of hands

 5 Minutes—Linemen: Snaking out of huddle to line of scrim-
        mage—charging
     Backs: Zig-zagging around spaced men

 5 Minutes—Ball recovery: Recover, recover and advance

15 Minutes—Review 5-man defenses—Add 5-4-2 (4 types)

10 Minutes—Line: Shivving on 7-man sled (Game mechanics)
     Backs and Ends: Passing and receiving drills

25 Minutes—New plays, review old ones

 5 Minutes—Fireman's carry

Finish: 220-yard dash

12:00	Lunch
12:45	Coaches meeting
2:00	Skull session
3:30	Squad in full dress on field (2 Hours)
3:30	Calisthenics and grass drills
3:40	Bags and tires
3:45	Wind sprints
3:55	Dashes
4:00	Linemen: Mechanics and skills

  (a) Pulling out drill on dummies and aprons
  (b) Shivving (on each other)
  (c) Ends crashing and drifting (bags)
  (d) Ends one handed passing
  (e) Line cross blocking
  (f) Pursuit (from 7-man sled)

Backs:
  (a) Zig-zag
  (b) Gauntlet
  (c) Hand-offs
  (d) Passing (on one knee)
  (e) Driving into bags
  (f) Practicing reverse hand-offs

TUESDAY

4:25	Linemen: Drills on 7-man sled
	Backs: Drills on charger-blocker and dummies
5:15	Shoulder to shoulder
5:20	Review 5-4-2 defenses, add 44, 46, 47, 48
5:40	Add new plays and review old ones
Finish:	220-yard dash
7:00–7:30	Short review of day's work

WEDNESDAY

8:00 A.M.	Coaches Meeting
9:00	Squad on field. Calisthenics and grass drills
9:10	Bag and tire drill
9:15	Wind sprints (3)
9:25	Dashes (two 220-yards)
9:30	Game skills and mechanics:

Backs:	Ends:	Centers:
Bucking gauntlet	One-hand passing	Long punt pass
Passing and	Receiving:	drill (weighted
receiving	Hook, hook and	ball)
(Flares, angles, de-	go,	Centering on Pass-
lays, stationary,	Burst of speed,	ing drill
hooks)	Change of pace,	
	Angle, Banana	

Linemen: Orientation and demonstration by line coach
12 Defensive Tactics:

(1) Sprinters charge
(2) Shiv
(3) Head stop
(4) Over
(5) Submarine
(6) Knife
(7) Free leg
(8) Split-by arms and butt
(9) Loop
(10) Bust thru
(11) Slant
(12) Roll-off

Also cover recognition of traps and screens

10:05   One-on-one pass defense—Backs and Ends (Skills and mechanics)

Line:Forming the pocket (Chicken Fighting)

10:15   Line: Cross body blocking on dummies

Backs: Ball handling drill—Dives, slants, cross bucks, delays, pitchouts

10:25   Timing practice on old and new plays

10:55   220-yard dash

Same noon schedule as Monday and Tuesday

3:30   Bag and tire drill

3:35   Calisthenics and grass drills

3:45   Three 220-yard dashes

3:55   Shoulder to shoulder

4:00   Backs: Gauntlet, ball handling of belly series, single wing

Line: Review traps and screens, roll-offs from double team

4:15   Line: (a) Pulling for traps, (b) Cross blocking (Use dummies and apron)

Backs: Diving between two held dummies (off the ground)

Ends: Crashing, steps, drifting, dropping back for pass defense

4:25   Line: Framework fundamentals—

(1) Essentials of line play, (2) double teaming, (3) post and drive, (4) high and low, (5) one on one, (6) blocking linebackers (cross and shoulder), (7) blocking stunters

Backs: Punting and receiving, P.A.T., field goal kicking. (Try to discover your backfield specialists. Teach skills of punting, etc.)

4:55   Line: Live two-on-one drill

Backs: Gauntlet tackling drill

5:05   Five-man tackling drill

5:25   Two 225-yard dashes

7:00–7:30 Review of day's activities

THURSDAY

8:00 A.M. Coaches Meeting

9:00   Squad on field. Calisthenics and grass drills

THURSDAY

9:10	Bag and tire drill
9:15	Wind sprints
9:25	Dashes (3)
9:35	Line:

Review offensive blocking—Post, drive, high and low, etc.

Backs:

Zig-zag drills, spinning drills, ball handling drills, driving into bags

Ends:

Review blocks, boxers shuffle, crashing, drifting, pass receiving

10:00	Whole squad on dummies and air aprons (blocking)
10:10	Defenses: Review four, five, and five-four—Add 62 tight and loose, 63, 63 slant and loop
10:40	Add New Plays. Practice for timing and finesse
11:00	220-yard dash

Regular noon schedule

3:30	Bag and tire drill
3:35	Calisthenics and grass drills
3:45	Three-man laterals (2)
3:55	One 220-yard dash
4:00	Review huddle and formation (with shifts if using single wing)
4:10	Guards, tackles, centers:

Review all blocking drills. Also defensive drills

Ends: Review all end drills

Backs: Review all running drills

4:40	Line on 7-man sled
	Backs on charger-blocker
4:50	Line on charger-blocker
	Backs on dummies
5:00	Punting orientation—Regular or spread—Proper protection and coverage
5:15	Shoulder to shoulder
5:20	One-on-one tackling gauntlet
5:30	One-on-one blocking drill
5:40	100-yard dash
7:00 P.M.	Short skull session to review day's work

FRIDAY

8:00 A.M.	Coaches Meeting
9:00	Squad on field. Calisthenics and grass drills
9:10	Bag and tire drill
9:15	Wind sprints
9:25	Dashes
9:35	Line:

        Work on defensive tactics

        Backs:

        Work on handoffs, belly plays, gauntlet

        Ends:

        Crashing, charge and drift, dropping back, shuffle
Backs and ends:

        Passing and receiving with one-on-one pass defense

| 10:00 | Point after Touchdown Orientation (Framework fundamentals) |
| 10:10 | Kickoffs—Coverage and receiving (Framework fundamentals) |

        Up the middle, sides, and reverse

10:30	Punt review
10:40	Plays
11:00	Two 220-yard dashes

Regular noon schedule

3:30	Bag and tire drill
3:35	Calisthenics and grass drills
3:45	3—220-yard dashes
3:55	Defenses: 71 (7 Diamond), 74 (7 Umbrella)
4:10	One-on-one blocking gauntlet
	One-on-one tackling gauntlet
4:30	Live punting scrimmage: Defense rushing, offense protecting and covering
4:45	P.A.T. scrimmage
4:55	Kickoff scrimmage
5:10	Two-on-one scrimmage (backs used as wingbacks or flankers)
5:25	Shoulder to shoulder
5:30	220-yard dash
7:00 P.M.	Meeting to review day's work

SATURDAY

One Practice only. General review.

9:00	Calisthenics and grass drills
9:10	Wind sprints
9:20	Dashes (2)
9:25	Review all defenses to date
9:50	Review all offensive and defensive drills and tactics
10:20	Line: on sled and charger-blocker
	Backs: on charger-blocker, dummies and review plays
10:40	Triangle play run-offs (coach observes all teams in play rehearsal)
11:00	Controlled scrimmage
11:25	Brief critique—220-yard dash—Dismiss squad for weekend

Second Week—Timing and Proficiency Drills

MONDAY

8:00 A.M.	Coaches Meeting
9:00	Players on field. Calisthenics and grass drills
9:10	Bag and tire drill
9:15	Wind sprints (3 times length of field—660 yards)
9:25	Dashes (two 220 yards)
9:35	Defenses: 8 man—Gap 8 and 83, spread defenses
10:00	Review all defenses
10:25	Review all plays
10:55	Two 220-yard dashes

Regular noon schedule

3:30	Calisthenics and grass drills
3:40	Bag and tire drill
3:45	Speed tests by position
4:00	Defense: 92 (9-man line) (11-man line) (Goal Line)
4:15	Line: Trap blocking (on 2 bags)
	Centers blocking on backer-ups
	Backs and Ends: Passing and receiving
4:25	Line: Gauntlet
	Backs: Gauntlet tackling drill
4:40	Punt blocking (4 ways) rough

5:00	Circle blocking drill
5:15	Lane tackling drill
5:25	880 Conditioning run
7:00 P.M.	Brief review of day's activities

TUESDAY

8:00 A.M.	Coaches meeting
9:00	Players on field. Calisthenics and grass drills
9:10	Bag and tire drill
9:15	Wind sprints (660 yards)
9:25	Two 220-yard dashes
9:35	Line:

    (a) Charging—On different signals
    (b) Chicken fighting for pass pocket
    (c) Trap drills
    (d) Cross blocking on dummies
    (e) Pursuit from 7-man sled

Ends:
    (a) Charging with line on *a* above
    (b) End drills—Slashing on dummies, 3 steps, drift-
        ing, dropping back, staying with flare man
    (c) Receiving (with backs *d* below)

Backs:
    (a) Ball handling drills—Handoffs and cutting right
        or left
    (b) Diving into bags
    (c) Diving over bags (into four men's arms)
    (d) Passing, receiving, man-for-man defense (with
        ends)

10:00	Fireman's carry (everybody)
10:10	Review four man defenses
10:25	Add new plays, review old ones
10:55	Two 220-yard Dashes

Regular noon schedule

3:30	Calisthenics and grass drills
3:40	Bag and tire drill
3:45	Wind sprints (220 yards on staggered signals)
3:55	Fireman's carry

TUESDAY

4:00	Shoulder to shoulder
4:05	Line on sled
	Backs on C-B, dummies
4:25	Line: Forming the pocket scrimmage
	Backs: Secondary tackling drill
4:40	Pursuit scrimmage
4:55	Pass scrimmage: forming pocket, pass defense
5:10	Controlled scrimmage
5:25	880-yard run
7:00	Short critique

WEDNESDAY

Note: It is the trend today in scholastic and collegiate circles to hold the first full scale pre-season scrimmage with some other school on this date. If such is the case, morning practice should be cancelled. A skull session for review purposes would be in order.

If no inter-school scrimmage is scheduled, it is recommended that the squad be given the morning off to rest and to break the drudgery of two-a-day practice sessions. A break will renew enthusiasm. A recommended practice is outlined for those coaches requiring practice.

9:00	Calisthenics and grass drills
9:10	Bag and tire drill
9:15	Wind sprints (660 yards)
9:25	Review all defense
10:00	Review all plays—Triangle
10:30	One Dash (220 yards)

Regular noon schedule

If game scrimmage is scheduled get ready for it. Otherwise schedule a full intra-squad scrimmage.

3:30	Calisthenics and grass drills
3:45	Bag and tire-drill
3:50	Wind sprints (220 yards)
4:00	Scrimmage
5:30	220-yard dash
7:00	Scrimmage critique

THURSDAY

8:00 A.M. Coaches meeting
9:00 Squad on field. Calisthenics and grass drills
9:10 Bag and tire drill
9:15 Wind Sprints (660 yards)
9:25 Dashes (Two 440 yards)
9:35 Review kick-offs—Receiving and blocking plus kicking off and coverage
9:45 Review punt blocking and punt coverage
10:00 Line: Trap blocking on dummies
　　　　　　Cross blocking on aprons
　　　　Backs and Ends: Passing and Receiving against three deep secondary defense (not rough)
10:20 Review Plays and add new ones
10:55 Finish with 2 dashes, 220 yards each

Regular noon schedule

3:30 Calisthenics and Grass Drills
3:40 Bag and tire drill
3:45 Wind Sprints (on staggered signals) 220 yards
3:55 Speed tests by position (25, 50, and 100 yards tests)
4:00 Line: Sled, charger-blocker, dummies
　　　　Backs: Charger-blocker, dummies, sled
4:40 Line: 3-on-1, 5-on-2 Drills
　　　　Backs: Secondary tackling drill
5:00 Whole squad: 3-on-3 sideline blocking—tackling drill
5:15 5 man Blocking—Tackling drill
5:30 880-yard run
　　　　No evening meeting

FRIDAY

8:00 A.M. Coaches meeting
9:00 Squad on field. Calisthenics and grass drills
9:10 Bag and tire drill
9:15 Wind sprints (on staggered signals) 440 yards
9:25 Speed tests—two 25, two 50, two 100-yard sprints
9:40 Line: Review all defensive and offensive tactics
　　　　Ends: Will review with line and also their own drills
　　　　Backs: Ball handling drills, zig-zag, gauntlet, pass defense, passing and receiving

FRIDAY

10:10	Punting daisy chain
	Kick-off—Reverse return daisy chain
10:30	Plays
10:55	Finish with 2 dashes 220 yards each

Regular noon schedule

3:30	Calisthenics and grass drills
3:40	Bag and tire drill
3:45	Wind sprints (660 yards)
3:55	Review all defenses against your running plays
4:30	Passing drill with receivers being hit on the line (Passer has 5 seconds to get off pass. No interior linemen. Guards and tackles line up opposite ends. Centers act as linebackers. 3 deep secondary)
5:00	Pursuit drill
5:15	Daisy chain scrimmage
5:30	880-yard run
	No evening session

SATURDAY

8:00 A.M.   Coaches meeting

There are few schools or colleges today who do not have a scrimmage scheduled with some other school. If such is not the case, then a full two hour "knock 'em down—drag 'em out" scrimmage should be in order. This scrimmage should in a large measure determine your squad and especially your varsity starters.

A morning or afternoon scrimmage is purely a matter of personal philosophy. It is Saturday. Kids have chores, etc.; college boys would like to get home for the weekend or just rest. It is recommended that you conduct a morning session and give the kids the afternoon off. If at camp, use the afternoon to break camp and travel. The boys will be anxious to get home.

A scheduled inter-school scrimmage will have to be held in the afternoon unless traveling distance is short.

FINAL GAME PREPARATIONS

MONDAY

The pre-season (pre-school) two-a-day practice sessions are completed. Classes are now in session which means only one evening practice. Coaches meetings must now be arranged according to class schedules. Often times they must be held after practice. Skull sessions must also be arranged during evening hours and, therefore, should be limited. The greatest majority of schools open their season's schedule after three weeks of practice. This week's practice program is based upon this premise. After school practice may vary from one to two hours. The following activities are timed for two hours. Squad on field at 4:00 P.M.

4:00   Calisthenics and Grass Drills
4:10   Line:
        (a) sled-dummies (10)
        (b) gauntlet (5)
        (c) shoulder to shoulder (5)
        (d) trap drills (5)
        (e) line blocking drills (5)
        (f) circle blocking drill (5)
        (g) forming pass pocket 7 on 7 (5)
        (h) two-on-one (with roll-offs) (10)
        (i) one-on-one (10)

    Backs:
        (a) dummies—charger-blocker (10)
        (b) one-on-one pass drill (10)
        (c) short yardage drills (hitting bags and diving) (10)
        (d) reverse drills (5)
        (e) circle blocking drill (5)
        (f) two-on-one tackling drill—ball carrier, blocker, safetyman (10)
        (g) passing drill with ends (10)
5:10   Whole squad: scrimmage mistakes ironed out
5:25   Basic defense with alternatives outlined for first opponent
    Orientation on first opponent
5:40   Run through Bread and Butter plays against opponent's favorite defense or defenses

MONDAY

6:00   880-yard run
7:00   Skull session
        Information on first opponent covered

TUESDAY

4:00   Calisthenics and grass drills
        (Jayvees work on opponent's chief plays especially pass
        patterns)
4:10   Line:
            (15)   sled (with pursuit drills)
            (5)   starts on staggered signals
            (15)   3 on 1
            (10)   5 on 2
        Ends: End drills

        Backs:
            (15)   charger-blocker, dummies
            (10)   secondary tackling drill
            (10)   pass defense with ends
            (10)   run backfield play patterns
4:55   Dummy defense against jayvees to get idea of opponents
        plays
5:25   Run all plays against defense (line give moderate resist-
        ance especially when forming the pass pocket)
5:55   880-yard run

WEDNESDAY

NOTE: If game is scheduled for Friday, scrimmage should be held
on Tuesday or Limited.

4:00   Calisthenics and grass drills
4:10   Line: Review offensive blocking, defensive tactics
        Backs: Blocking on dummies, pass defense drills, run
            plays for timing
        Jayvee team: Drill on opponent's plays
4:40   Defensive scrimmage against jayvees
5:10   Offensive scrimmage
5:50   880-yard run

Thursday

4:00	Calisthenics and grass drills
4:10	Line: Drills—Charging on staggered signals, pulling out of line, trapping drills, screen pass drill, roll-out drills, sled drill
	Backs: Ball handling drills, driving between bags, diving for one yard, pass defense, charge-blocker
4:40	Review opponent: (a) Offensive strength (pet plays, trick plays, pass patterns—run by jayvees)
	(b) Defenses opponent may use
5:10	Run own plays against bags varying defenses
5:45	Shoulder to shoulder
5:50	Fireman's carry
5:55	880-yard run
7:00	Skull session

Friday

4:00	Calisthenics and grass drills
4:10	Two dashes (440 yards)
4:15	Review:
	(1) P.A.T.
	(2) Kick-offs
	(3) punts—blocking punts and coverage
4:45	Last minute details for game:
	(1) basic defense and multiple continuities
	(2) opponent's chief plays
	(3) opponent's possible defenses
	(4) offensive plays to combat these defenses
	(Review opponent's possible weaknesses)
5:10	Triangle offensive review (all plays)
5:45	Short pep talk
5:50	One dash (220 yards)

SUMMARY

The small college coach and his practice schedule can right-fully be labeled as the liaison program between the high schools and the major colleges. Because of the mixture of player talent ranging from a blue-chip boy or two, the typical small college calibre, to the boy with little or no experience the small college coach must plan his practice sessions to provide the necessary drills to develop inexperienced personnel and at the same time meet the needs of the veteran boy on his squad. Often he must carry out his program under many limiting factors which are typical to many small colleges who have curtailed their athletic programs from one of public consumption to a campus activity whereby it becomes a supplement to the students' over-all curricular development. The program must be planned for a limited staff and limited player personnel with the assumption that the team has little knowledge of the techniques of the game. Time is of an essence so the greatest economy is demanded in planning the practice sessions. Because of late classes and dining room regulations the time available is often limited to sixty-minutes which poses a problem in planning the contents of the practice session and still finding time for the specialist to get his specialities completed. Such conditions make it mandatory that the small college coach plan the best possible practice schedule in advance of the season with recognition that changes can be made without impairing the effectiveness of the total practice plan.

8

THE LARGE COLLEGE
PRE-SEASON PRACTICE PLAN

Complete Organization a Requisite

A close similarity exists between the major college program and the large high school program. Larger staffs, more player personnel, extra time, more specialization, greater facilities, and more emphasis upon winning with its accompanying pressure dictate a program organized to every minute detail. While the success of any football team is dependent upon complete organization whether it be small high school or small college there is a difference in the enormity of the organization. The limitations faced by the small schools prohibit a smooth, over-all organization. Limited staffs, time, teaching load, late classes put many harassing stumbling blocks in the way of complete organization by small schools. The major colleges in the main have the necessary time, the staff, money for equipment, men, managers, publicity staffs, and a well-rounded recruitment program. The head coach picks his staff and has everything in his favor which puts his proverbial head on the block with the win or else ultimatum.

Each Work Day Involves Long Hours and a Challenge

With their jobs at stake the head coach and his staff must spend hours upon hours in organizational meetings. More work is done in the coach's office than on the field. In many of the major colleges the coaching staff does not do any teaching. Their jobs are strictly football; sixteen-hour days are not uncommon during the season. It is small wonder that many major college coaches have nervous breakdowns, ulcers, and other such occupational disorders. It causes a person to wonder why coaches accept or vie for perhaps the most pressurized jobs in our country. For some it is the higher salary; however, tenures may be short. For others it represents the glamour of the "Big Time." To the majority it issues a challenge to excel in a chosen profession with prestige a great compensating factor.

Organization Entails Supervision and Delegation of Work

The chief responsibility of the major college coach is organization and supervision of his program with delegation of duties and responsibilities to his staff. He delegates most, if not all, functional work to his aides. The staff will be divided into a line coach, backfield coach, quarterback coach, defensive coach, and a freshmen team staff. Some schools may have additional coaches to the ones named above, while others may have one or more less coaches. Each man has special functions to perform from the simple individual drills through combination drills, team cohesion drills and on to specialities. Each man is an expert in his functional work and is directly responsible to the head coach. The latter has organized all phases of the program on paper with the aid of his staff prior to practice. On the field he may walk around the practice field supervising, observing groups at work, making corrections, or he may stand on a platform with a megaphone in hand and issue orders, instructions, or make notes for the next staff meeting. He normally takes over full command of the team during combination drills and scrimmages. There are times when he may not even appear for a practice session due to the many details he must execute in the way of preparation for chalk talks, evaluating movies, the scouting report, interviews, publicity work, etc. In such cases he must depend entirely upon his staff to carry out his program. Major college football is an enormous program and as such demands complete staff cooperative effort. It is in such a program that the old axiom bears weight—good assistants are the arms and legs of the head coach.

Field Organization

There is no wasted time once practice is called into session. The field is marked off into areas to which squad personnel report. Coaches are present to direct the work prescribed for that specific area. The players will move from area to area working on their primary functions which evolve from warm ups, individual drills, everyday drills and on into combination drills where framework fundamentals of offense and defense take shape from the simple introduction through game simulated conditions. Timing, poise, and finesse are emphasized.

Most Work Performed by Small Groups

If you check the two major college programs sampled for this chapter you will readily see that most of the work is done by small player groups performing specialities peculiar to their individual positions which when combined into squad work will unite all phases of the system into a cohesive team effort. The reason for group work is that assistant coaches can offer better supervision. The Air Force Academy program lists such group work as: a group on the chute drill while another is on the 7-man sled and another on agility and reaction drills. The guards and tackles jump over to trap drills while the ends plus backs engage on roll up blocks and 2 on 1. You will find backs in sets drilling on plays and pass protection while the guards, tackles, ends and centers will be performing various line drills related to their individual position. Each group is directed by a coach performing definite functions even when groups are combined in drills. For example, backs and ends working on pass patterns will be supervised by a coach concerned only with that phase of work while another coach will concern himself with the function of pass defense from the various defensive alignments comprising the team's defensive repertory.

A Sample of Inter-Related Staff Functioning

To get a clearer picture of such inter-related staff functioning check the Penn State practice program for Monday and Tuesday of the third week. Here you can see the names of Pat, Joe,

J.T., Earl, Tor, etc. each of which signifies an assistant coach. The coaches are working with definite groups either offensively or with defensively simulated conditions (Jacks). Every player and coach is actively engaged in some phase of the total team program. No one is sitting around idle. The coaches are physically and mentally alert to their duties and will catch the slightest deviation or mistake.

On other days you will notice: *(Jim)—Blue & Green on 54 defense—7 on 7, Rush Pass, Pursuit,* which means that the coach, Jim, is working designated Blue and Green teams on defense practicing rushing the passer and pursuit. The Red and White teams under Tor, nickname for Torretti, are practicing offensive three and five traps against odd and even defenses. These teams may comprise a whole team, a line, or just the players concerned with this phase of the work. Each player is practicing skills peculiar to his position which could include individual offensive or defensive calls that are required of Penn State tackles and ends. These drills are related to the Penn State offensive and defensive philosophy. You have drills which are peculiar to your program. Do not imitate, but substitute your own drills, if you adopt any phase of the Penn State program.

Scrimmage

Even during scrimmage no player personnel is sitting idly by. Before practice every player is identified with a designated team which may be called Red, White, Blue, Green or team 1, team 2, 3, 4, 5, etc. Each time is slated for either offensive or defensive scrimmage or a combination of both. Any extra personnel will be assigned to a Jacks drill that may call for certain defensive maneuvers under simulated conditions, or other purposeful results.

While teams 1 and 3 scrimmage team 5 offensively, interchanging every 15 minutes, team 2 will be scrimmaging team 4 defensively also switching from offense to defense. Coaches will be carrying out assigned duties throughout the scrimmages.

Penn State uses a motivating device on their first Saturday full-scale scrimmage. The scrimmage lasts 45 minutes. The winner is rewarded by being allowed to go to the showers. This instills early season alertness, spirit, and aggressiveness.

Off-Field Activities

These activities, so vital to the success of the major college program are too numerous and detailed to cover in this chapter; however, it must be stated again that most of the planning and organizational work is done prior to the daily practice. Practice, actually represents but a small portion of the time element making up the coach and his staff's working day.

A. Movies

Countless hours are spent by the staff as a group and individually in checking plus evaluating game movies. Some schools even shoot movies of their practices. Players are graded individually by position offensively and defensively. Quite often movies are run over dozens of times with the staff looking for that one little escapable flaw that could measure the difference between victory and defeat. Commentaries must be prepared to brief the team in viewing the movies. Mistakes must be remembered when the assistants cover the movies with small groups so they may be brought to the attention of the individual player. Movies are so important to the major college coach and yet very time-consuming. Many a coach has been known to jump out of bed just to check some segment of a game movie because of a subconscious thought or an idea. Few major coaches or their assistants sleep with anything but football on their mind. It is a 24-hour-a-day chore.

B. Chalk Talks

Many coaches hold at least one chalk session daily and some few even hold two, one before practice and one in the evening. Every detail must be organized for the most efficient dissemination since the boys do have class work which also demands their time. The preparation for the players meetings takes time of both head coach and his assistants. Quite often the talks and diagramming are covered by every member of the staff. The range covers information from negating mistakes, new offensive plays, changes in defensive alignments, the scouting report, recognizing the opponent's strength and weaknesses, new plans for the opponent, movie review, announcements, and a pep talk.

C. Staff Meetings

Staff meetings are a daily requirement including Saturday and Sunday. It is at these sessions that a meeting of the minds takes place which includes every phase of the total football program: evaluation of a squad personnel, practice, the scouting report, movies, new ideas, the opponent, demands by alumni or the administration, public relations, and recruiting. These meetings produce the harmonious agreement that is reflected in the success on the field. Again staff meetings as other off-field activities are time consuming. Yet, any major staff will quickly agree that irregular working hours are the price of success. These meetings may start at 7:30 A.M. and continue until lunch. After lunch another meeting may be held or movies shown to the squad. After-lunch meetings may be the prelude preparation for the afternoon meeting. After practice another brief meeting may be held in preparation to the regular evening squad meeting. Afterwards movies may again be reviewed thus easily giving credence to the 16-hour working day. It is a known fact that former Notre Dame coach, Frank Leahy, had a couch in his office and rarely got home during the week. The December 4, 1959, issue of the *Notre Dame Football Review,* Vol. 101, No. 9, carried an article called "Coaches' Week—From Monday to Sunday" which described in detail Coach Joe Kuharich's work week. The article is too long to quote here, but it did follow the trend established earlier in this paragraph. Coach Kuharich's day usually began with an early morning meeting at 7:30 A.M. and lasted until 10:00 P.M. (It did not elaborate beyond 10:00 P.M.) or 14½ hours of steady work.

D. Recruiting

Recruiting does not wait until the season is over. Alumni and high school coaches are continuously recommending boys.

While the head coach does not attend to the details, he must assign an assistant to this important chore, and he must be on hand to greet the boys and exhibit his interest. Seats are provided on the field along with the regular players bench where the prospective athlete is honored as a guest. Follow-up contact must be maintained with likely prospects.

E. Other Functions

The off-field activities are covered in Chapter 10; however, the ones treated in this chapter were those that pertain positively to the major college coach. There are countless others, all time consuming, such as scouting assignments, public relations, which entail speaking engagements, appearing at Downtown Quarterback Club Meetings, Lion's Club, etc.

Major College Practice Program Offers Many New Ideas

While this book is chiefly aimed for the high school coach, the major college program is presented for the benefit of that segment among the high school ranks who may aspire to major college status. The programs will offer some idea on the organization and type of practice activities conducted by the major college coach. It may also reveal ideas that can be incorporated into your own practice programs. To the small high school coach it may serve as a fine example of practice organization. The terminology may vary and perhaps not be understood in some cases; however, this should not discourage the reader since such terms as *stunt, blitz, fire, blow, shoot,* etc., may mean the same thing or vary in different sections of the country on the different school levels. Close scrutiny of the activities will help in diagnosing the intent or clarify interpretation. For example, refer to the Penn State practice schedule for Wednesday afternoon of the first week from 5:10 to 5:30 P.M. You will notice three groups at work; one involves the backs and ends in a live drill which could cover pass offense and defense, wide running plays such as the slant, roll-out, sweep, and option; the middle group finds guards and centers opposing each other in what could be one on one, traps, or pass pocket formation;

group number three involves guards, tackles, and centers who are practicing splits, pass rushing defense, and traps. It could also include the Oklahoma 5 on 3 drills. You can visualize what drills of your own could fit the situation or which of the ones you are observing could fit into your football scheme of activities.

Two Major College Programs Presented

This chapter presents the programs of two of the most successful coaches in the game today—namely, Ben Martin, head coach of the United States Air Force Academy, and Charles "Rip" Engle, head coach at Penn State University. The author feels highly indebted to both gentlemen for the fine spirit of cooperation in contributing material contained in this chapter. Space prohibits detailed explanations and in order to offer a sampling of both programs only the first week of the Air Force Academy's schedule will be presented. The programs for the first and second week cover the major teaching phases involving conditioning and fundamentals; while the third week is designed to perfect timing, poise and details in addition to orient ing the squad on the strengths and weaknesses of the first opponent and the preparation for that opponent.

Uniqueness of Penn State Daily Practice Sheet

Rip Engle, the venerable Penn State Coach, has a unique way of keeping tab on his personnel and dividing his work into categories. He distributes a daily mimeographed practice schedule to each member of his staff. At the bottom of each sheet there is enough space available for a listing of all players who will be free for practice, those with late classes, and those who are on the sick or disabled list. The trainer supplies the latter information while the former data is taken from a master sheet of all personnel. Thus each assistant knows what players they will have available for the workout which allows them to group them for everyday drills, individual drills, combination drills, and team drills. On the upper right hand corner of each daily practice sheet Engle lists new activities for introduction and practice for that particular day.

Breakdown of Penn State Practice

Each Penn State practice is subdivided into seven definite categories with time limits for each. By checking the first few days of practice you will notice them to be:

5 minutes	Warm ups—Individual calisthenics
10 minutes	Everyday drills—Agility, Reaction, Snappy blocking and tackling for feel
15 minutes	Individual drills—Drills peculiar to position such as 2 on 1, 1 on 1, pass defense, etc.
35 minutes	Combination drills—By groups: whole line, guards, tackles, centers, sets (backs) Backs and ends . . . pass patterns, defense, forming pocket, traps, etc.
35 minutes	Team drills—defense, offense, punting, THUD, running plays against defense, light, mild resistance or scrimmage
10 minutes	Conditioning—drills that involve running such as punt coverage, sprints, from formation (starts), etc.
15 minutes	Specialities—backs and ends passing and receiving, punting, kickoffs, point after touchdown, field goals, stunting, guards pulling, tackles on calls, etc.

In checking positions Penn State labels left halfbacks as A; right halfbacks as X; fullback as B; and the quarterback as Q.

It might also be added that both Penn State and the Air Force Academy face many of the problems prevalent among the small colleges. Entrance requirements and scholastic standards are high with no concessions to the athlete. Time is also a factor, especially at the Air Force Academy. Both schools find late classes and laboratory periods do interfere with practice time. Nonetheless, the records of the two schools attest to fine organization based upon a well-constructed practice program. For your personal evaluation the two programs are here presented.

AIR FORCE ACADEMY

Pre-Season Football Practice

FIRST WEEK

I. Introduction

Here at the Academy we have to utilize every minute of pre-season practice time because we are unable to practice twice a day, and we are limited to one hour and forty-five minutes each day on the field.

We feel that we get the most out of our practice time by working in small groups under a highly organized and efficient practice schedule.

II. Main Objectives of Pre-Season.

A. Player Evaluation:
   1. Identify the best football players.

B. Fundamental Skills:
   1. Blocking
   2. Tackling
   3. Running
   4. Passing
   5. Receiving
   6. Kicking
   7. Stance & Starts
   8. Exchange
   9. Snap Count.

C. Conditioning:
   1. Stretchers
   2. Bridges
   3. Set Ups
   4. Push Ups
   5. Leg Raisers
   6. Grass Drill
   7. Rocker
   8. Running

D. Team Work:
   1. Snap Count
   2. Dummy offense vs. 8 Shield Holders
   3. Dummy defense vs. Full Team
   4. Pass offense and Pass Pro

5. Pass defense with Backs, Ends, L.B.'s.
6. Kicking game spread, tight punt, field goals, extra points, quick kick.

WEEK'S PRACTICE SCHEDULE

Monday

1600–1605	Calisthenics
	Stretches, push ups, set ups, bridges, grass drill
1605–1610	Backs and Line Snap Count
1610–1625	*Drill Period*
	A. *Halfbacks* Offense

Switch 7½ Minutes

Handoff, Daylight Drills

B. *Halfbacks* Defense
Roll, hitting-position, flipper
Roll, hitting-position, tackle

C. *Line* (Three Groups)

5 Minutes each.

Chute Drill
Agility and Reaction
Sled (7-Man)

1625–1645	*Backs* Offense
	A. Chute, Roll up dummies

10 Minute switch.

Backs Defense

B. One-on-One, Two-on-One, Hash Mark Drill
Line (4 groups)
10 Minutes, One-on-One
10 Minutes, Prone, roll, chug, wave (Reaction and Agility)

1645–1705	A. *Backs* and *Ends* Pass Patterns

Switch 10 Minutes

B. *Backs* and *Ends*. L.B's, Pass Defense
Line (Two Groups)
G's, C's, T's
Pulling vs. Stand up dummies
Triangle, Circle, Prone
(Contact drills)

1705–1735	7 Three-on-Three Oklahoma Drills
1735–1745	Shuttle Race (Divide the Squad)

Tuesday

1600–1605	Calisthenics
1605–1610	Backs and Line Snap Count
1610–1625	*Backs* Offense
	Handoff, Daylight, Gauntlet

Switch 7½ Minutes.

Backs Defense
Roll, hitting-position, flipper, drills
Roll, hitting-position, Tackle
Face Off

1610–1625	*Line*

5 Minutes each

Chute Drills
Agility and Reaction
Sled (7-Man)

1625–1645	*Backs* Offense

Switch 10 Minutes.

Backs in sets
Backs Defense
Defensive positioning
Line

4 groups 10 Minutes each
Hooking, one-on-one, Prone Drill

1645–1700	*Backs* and *Ends*

Roll up blocks, two-on-one
Line

3 Groups, three-on-one
two-on-one

1700–1730	7 Groups, three-on-three Oklahoma Drills
1730–1745	Squad Divides into two Groups.
	Group I —Offensive Scrim
	Group II—Defensive Scrim

Wednesday

1600–1605	Calisthenics
1605–1610	Snap Count
1610–1630	*Backs* Offense

Switch 10 Minutes.

Backs in Sets
Backs Defense
Roll, hitting-position, flipper

    Roll, hitting-position, tackle
    Intercept Drill
    Line (Three Groups)
    Chute Drill
    Sled (7-Man)
    Agility and Reaction

1630–1650 *Backs* Two Groups
  Switch 10 Minutes.
    Group I —Three-on-one
    Group II—Defensive Alignment
    Line Drills
    G & C Trap Drill
    Three-on-one Wing Backs

1650–1715 *Backs* and *Ends* Offense
    Widening Drill (Defense)
    Pass Patterns
    Backs Defense
    Defensive alignment
    Line (Two Groups)
    Group I —Pass Pro Plays
    Group II—Hit Drill Prone

1715–1745 Offensive Scrim.
    Groups 1 and 3 vs. 5
  Switch each 15 Minutes

1715–1745 Defensive Scrim
    Group 2 vs. 4

Thursday

1600–1605 Calisthenics
1605–1610 Snap Count
1610–1640 Defensive Skeleton Drill vs. Team
  Switch Each 10 Minutes.
    Backs, LB's, T's, Ends
    Backs in Sets
    G's and C's
    Traps, One-on-One

1640–1710 *Backs* Offense
  Switch 10 Minutes.
    Roll up blocks with Ends
    Backs Defense
    Pass Defensive adjustments

Thursday

1710–1730	*Offensive Scrim*
	Group 1 and 3 vs. 5
	Defensive Scrim
	Group 2 vs. 4
1730–1745	Switch Groups

Friday

1600–1605	Calisthenics
1605–1610	Snap Count
1610–1640	Defensive Skeleton Drill
	Backs, Ends, LB's, T's

Switch each 10 minutes.

Pass Offense Backs and Ends

Line

Pass Pro

1640–1720	*Kicking Game* Two Groups
	Group I —Tight punt and Spread Punt

Switch 20

Kickoff, extra point

Group II—Punt Return and Kick Off Return

Punt Block

1720–1745	*Dummy Offense* and *Defense*

Switch 12½.

Group 1 and 3 vs. 5

Group 2 vs. 4

Saturday

Game Scrimmage

1430–1630	Group 1 vs 3

30 Minutes on, 30 Minutes Off

Group 2 vs. 4

PENN STATE UNIVERSITY

Pre-Season Practice Schedule

Tuesday, A.M.

8:25– 8:30	As and Centers—Hand Ups
8:30– 8:35	*Warm Up*—(1) Jumping Jack (2) Toe Toucher
	(3) Push Up and Clap (4) Run and Drop
	(5) Stance and Starts

Everyday Drill 8:35– 8:55	*Backs*—(1) Wave (2) Shuffle (3) Hit-Hit (4) Half Speed Tackling (5) Down the line (6) Circle Drill *Line*—(1) Boards (2) Belly Slam (3) Half Speed Tackling (4) Bounce one (5) Somersault-Hit
Ind. Drills 8:55– 9:15	*Backs*—Offense—Dive Drill Defense—2 on 1 pass def. drill 10-10 —15 yards *Line*—Es—Ts, Gs—Cs—1 on 1 Instruction then full—2 on 1—VS (Game)
Comb. Drills 9:15– 9:50	*Line*—(15) Ind Drill on Calls and Rules—(20 Min) By Lines—Calls Play HB—QB—Drill *Backs*—Run on Line—*40, 41C, 42, 42 Option, Scissors, 40 Run or Pass*
9:50–10:25	Thud above plays by teams—VS—54—6-2 BLUE vs WHITE RED vs GREEN
10:25–10:35	*Backs*—Punt and Receive COVERED —Cover for Cond. *40 Series* *Line*—Take off on Sled *Punt Return* —(3 hits at a time) *Word Passes* *54 Defense*
10:35–10:45	Backs and E—Pass and Receive Continue Punt and Receive—Kick Off—Extra Points Gs—0, 1, 8, 7 Pull Ts—Calls

Tuesday, P.M.

4:00– 4:15	SPECIALTIES	Pass and Receive Punt and Receive—ExtraPoints —Kick Off LGs and Cs—Key and get to hook area Ts and RG—Rush Passer

Tuesday, P.M.

4:15– 4:20   Agility Drills—(1) Forward Run   (2) Backward Run   (3) Half Eagle   (4) Carioca
(5) Crab   (6) Bridge   (7) Figure 8

4:20– 4:35   *Backs*—(1) Wave   (2) Somersault and Hit
(3) Shuffle   (4) Angle interception   (5) Balance
Tackle
Line—(1) Boards   (2) Balance Tackle   (3) Hit
—Hit   (4) Bounce and Shuffle   (5) Wave

4:35– 4:55   *Backs*   (10)   2 on 1 Pass Defense—20 Yards
(10)   (A and X)—Calls and 40, 48 Pass—
(B and Q) 42, 42 Option, 40
Es—54 Key (10) Pass Defense (10)
Ts and RG—Deliver Defensive blow and React
—54 and 45
BUs—Key Drill VS Runs

4:55– 5:30   *Backs and 1 Center*—(17) Play HB—QB—(17) 40
Series—Add—43 CT—41 Power—43 Trap
Line—Blue and Green—(Jim) 54 Defense—7 on
7, Pass Rush, Pursuit (17 and Switch)
Red and White—(Tor)—3 and 5 Trap VS Odd
and Even

5:30– 5:45   *Backs and Es*—Word Passes
Line—Word Pass Protection

5:45– 6:05   Thud by Teams
6:05– 6:15   Punt and Punt Return

Wednesday, A.M.

New: 60–30 Passes

BACKS	LINE
8:30–8:35	8:30–8:35
Warm Up	Warm Up
8:35–8:45	8:35–8:50
Everyday Drills	Everyday Drills
(1) Wave (2) Shuffle	(1) Boards (2) Belly Slam
(3) Hit—Hit (4) Half	(3) Hit—Hit—Hit
Speed Tackling	(4) Somersault and Hit

BACKS	LINE

8:45–9:15
Individual Drills
(10) 2 on 1 Pass Defense
   LH   RH
(20) A and X
  (1) 30s–60s Passes
  (2) Calls
  (3) Word Passes
    FB   GB
    B and QB
  (1) 30s–60s
  (2) 42 and 46 Option
  (3) Word Passes

8:50–9:15
Individual Drills
Es–Calls–Pass Patterns
30–60
Def. 54 Blow, Blitz,
Fire, 1-on-1
Gs and C–1-on-1 as BU or
head on
2-on-1
Pass Protection–Word and
Roll Out
1 (7) Plays
Ts–Calls
Split Rule
1-on-1
Pass Protection and
Pass Rush

Combination Drills

9:15– 9:30   { *Backs*–Play QB, HB–Drill–Field position
               Line–Team Defenses–Blow, Blitz, Fire

9:30– 9:50   { *Backs and Ends*–60 and 30 Passes
Drill 5   *Int. Line*–60 Passes–30 Passes–Protection

Team Drills

9:50–10:20   Thud–Runs and Passes–VS 54–All maneuvers
all formations but E over

Conditioning

10:20–10:30   { *Backs*–Ladder and Crowther
              Line–Sled and Ladder

10:30–10:45   { Gs–3 (5) Trap
Specialties and   Es–Word Passes and Releases
Challenge   Ts–Play Traps
                 Backs–Roll Out Passes and Word
                 Punt–Kick Off–Extra Point

Wednesday, P.M.

New: 41C Pass–41 CP–Es Left
          47C Pass–47 CP–Es Right

Wednesday, P.M.

4:00– 4:15   SPECIALTIES   {Running passes—40—48
Extra Points and Punt
Int. Line—Split rules and Games

4:15– 4:20   Agility Drills

BACKS

4:20–4:30
(1) Wave   (2) Shuffle
(3) Bounce
(4) Circle Interception

4:30–4:40
2 on 1 Pass Def.   20 Yards

4:40–4:55
X and A—Dive Drill
Counter Passes
Calls
B and Q—Dive Drill
Counter Passes
40—48

LINE

4:20–4:35
(1) Balance Tackle   (2) Half
Speed Tackle   (3) Wave
(4) Bounce one and shuffle
(5) Bounce (Point)

4:35–4:50
BUs—Forward and Retreat In-
terception and Tip Drill
Es—Split and Flanker Rule
and Pass Defense
Ts—Down field blocking drill
Pursuit
Rush Passer VS Roll Out to
and Away

4:55– 5:10   {Backs—Run on Lines
Line—Counter Passes and play by lines—
2 Groups

5:10– 5:30   Live Drill #6

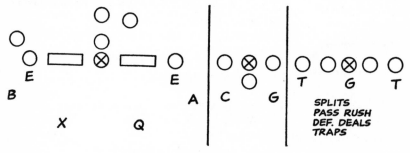

Fig. 21

5:30– 6:00   {Pass and run call situations
Quick kick to exchange ball
40s—30s—60s

6:00– 6:15   Punt return (0 men down–3 men down–
Teams cover)

Thursday, A.M.

NEW: Screen Rt–Left 3B
Draw Rt-Left–54 Rt–Lt–Gaps

BACKS	LINE
8:30–8:35 Warm Up	8:30–8:35 Warm Up
8:35–8:45 (1) Wave (2) Shuffle (3) Somersault (4) Bounce	8:35–8:50 Everyday Drills: (1) Boards (2) Hit–Hit–Hit (3) Bounce One (4) Somersault and Hit
8:45–8:55 2 on 1 Pass Defense	8:50–9:15 Ind. Drills E–T–G–C:
8:55–9:15	(1) 1 on 1 (2) 2 on 1

A and X $\left\{\begin{array}{l}\text{Call} \\ \text{Counter Pass} \\ \text{Blocks} \\ \text{Pass Protection}\end{array}\right.$

B and Q $\left\{\begin{array}{l}\text{Screens} \\ \text{30s–60s} \\ \text{40–48}\end{array}\right.$

$\left\{\begin{array}{l}\text{J.T.–1 Call} \\ \text{Jim–3 Call} \\ \text{Tor–3 (5)} \\ \quad\text{Trap}\end{array}\right.$

9:15– 9:30 $\left\{\begin{array}{l}\textit{Backs}–\text{Play QB–HB Drill–Hashmarks} \\ \textit{Line}–\text{Team defenses–Gap Rt and Left– 54 Rt} \\ \quad\text{and Left}\end{array}\right.$

9:30– 9:50 $\left\{\begin{array}{l}\textit{Backs}–\text{Run on Lines–2 Groups–Add 3 B} \\ \quad\text{(FB's)} \\ \textit{Line}–\text{By lines–Calls–Traps–Add 3 B–} \\ \quad\text{2 Groups VS 54–62}\end{array}\right.$

9:50–10:20   Thud–Red vs. White, Blue vs. Green

10:20–10:30 $\left\{\begin{array}{l}\textit{Backs}–\text{On Crowther} \\ \textit{Line}–\text{Sled–Take off then roll outs}\end{array}\right.$

10:30–10:45   SPECIALTIES $\left\{\begin{array}{l}\text{Punt–Throw–Extra Points} \\ \text{Kick Off} \\ \text{Ts and Gs–Screen and Draw} \\ \quad\text{Technique}\end{array}\right.$

Thursday, P.M.

4:00– 4:15   SPECIALTIES   { Punts, Extra Points—Pass
Kick Offs
Line—63 Defense

4:15– 4:20   Agility Drills

BACKS	LINE
4:20–4:30	4:20–4:35
(1) Balance Tackle	Everyday Drills:
(2) Hit–Hit (3) Tip Drill	(1) Balance Tackle
(4) Half Speed Tackle	(2) Wave
4:30–4:40	(3) Bounce (Pt.)
2 on 1 Pass Defense	(4) Half Speed Tackle
4:40–4:55	4:35–4:55

LH and RH { 40 R and P—
48 R and P
Dive Drill
30s—60s

BUs: Key Drill
RG-T: (1) Rush Passer
          (2) Pursuit
Es: Pass Defense

Q and FB { 42 and
42 Option
Dive Drill
Pass Pro-
tection

4:55– 5:15   { *Backs and Es*—Screens—Draws—41C Pass and
          Es Left—47C Pass and Es Rt
Int. Line—Draws and Screens—VS odd and even
          —Counter Passes

5:15– 5:35   Drill #2

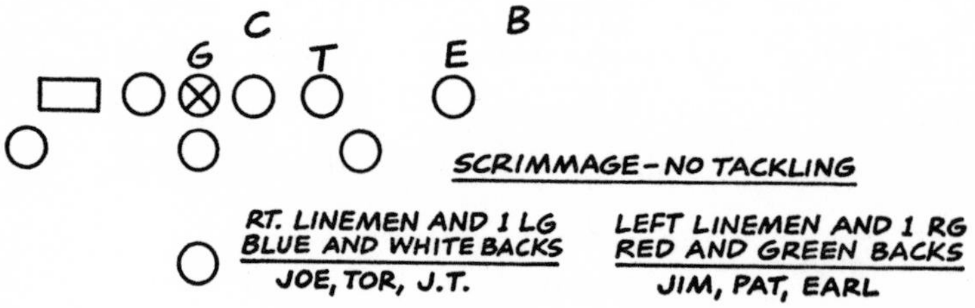

SCRIMMAGE – NO TACKLING

RT. LINEMEN AND 1 LG
BLUE AND WHITE BACKS
JOE, TOR, J.T.

LEFT LINEMEN AND 1 RG
RED AND GREEN BACKS
JIM, PAT, EARL

Fig. 22

5:35– 6:05   Thud—Blue vs. Green, Red vs. White
6:05– 6:15   Punt and Punt Return

Friday, A.M.

NEW:
95 Check Out
45 Defense
Test Mistakes

BACKS

8:30–8:35
Warm Up

8:35–8:45
(1) Wave   (2) Shuffle
(3) Hit   (4) Angle Interception

8:45–8:55
2 on 1 Pass Defense

8:55–9:15
A and X { Call
{ 40 R and P

B and Q { 42 and
{ 42 Option
{ 40 and 48

9:15– 9:35 { *Backs*—Flood Drill (Use of Thunder)
{ *Line* { Calls and Passes VS 54 Gaps—54R—Left
{ Jacks—Run Plays—Roll Out Rt—Lt
{ Drop Back

9:35–10:00

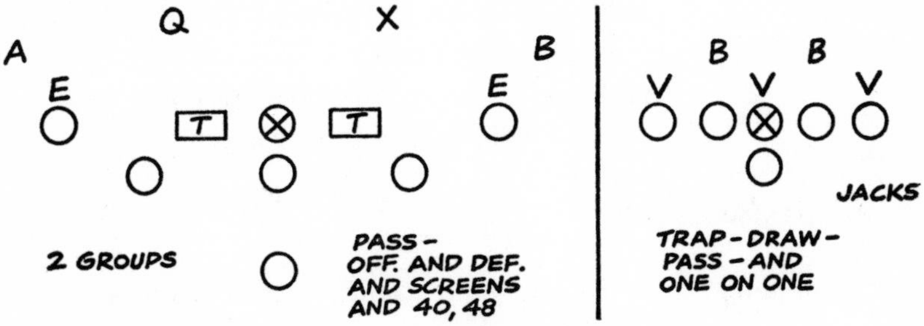

LINE

8:30–8:35
Warm Up

8:35–8:50
Everyday Drills
(1) Boards
(2) Hit—Hit and 1
(3) Bounce Shuffle
(4) Half Speed Tackle

8:50–9:15
Ind. Drills
T: Trap Reactions
E: 1-on-1, 2-on-1
G-C: (15) 3-on-3
(10) Traps VS
Odd-Even

2 GROUPS

PASS-OFF. AND DEF. AND SCREENS AND 40, 48

TRAP – DRAW – PASS – AND ONE ON ONE

JACKS

Fig. 23

10:00–10:20   Thud—42, 42 Option, 43T, 41C, Scissor Rt

10:20–10:30 { *Backs*—Ladder and Machines
{ *Line*—Sled—One Team at a time on Ladder

10:30–10:45   SPECIALTIES AND CHALLENGE—Kick Off

Friday, P.M.

4:00– 4:05	Agility	
4:05– 4:20	SPECIALTIES	Q Kick—Pass and Receive Ex. Pts. Punt

BACKS	LINE
4:20–4:30	4:20–4:35
(1) Hit, Hit	Everyday Drills
(2) Half Speed Tackling	(1) Wave (2) Somersault—
(3) Balance Tackle	Hit (3) Balance Tackle
(4) Interception	(4) Boards (5) Bounce (Pt)
4:30–4:40	4:35–4:55
2 on 1 Pass Defense	Ind. Drills
4:40–4:55	E: 45 Defense
	T: (1) Rush Passer
A and X { Pass Protection and Lane / 40–48 Run— / Pass	(2) 45 Defense
	G-C: (1) Draw Tech
	(2) 45–63 Defense

B and Q { Draws and Screens / Pass Protection

4:55– 5:15	*Backs*—Run on Lines all plays and Counter
	    Passes
	Line—Thud all plays—VS our defenses
	    2 Groups

5:15– 5:35	Blue vs. Green—3 Down Pass Scrim Red vs. White—Use Draw—Screen
5:35– 5:50	*Backs*—Color and White—Thunder *Line*—45 Defense
5:50– 6:05	Punt and Punt Return—4 men down—2 wide— 2 down middle
6:05– 6:15	Signals—10 yards in { Accurate Line up Accurate Huddle and Break Hold Points Take Off and Run

Saturday, A.M.

NEW:
40 Auto
Extra Points
63 Fire
Rev 54—45

BACKS	LINE
8:30–8:35	8:30–8:35
Warm Up	Warm Up
8:35–8:45	8:35–8:50
(1) Wave (2) Shuffle	Everyday Drills
(3) Bounce Shuffle	(1) Boards (2) Bounce
(4) Tip Drill	Shuffle (3) Wave
8:45–8:55	(4) Balance Tackle
2-on-1 Pass Defense	
8:55–9:15	8:50–9:15
A and X—Dive Drill Calls	Ind. Drills: E–T–G–C
B and Q—Dive Drill	Review Defenses
30 and 60s	
42 and 42 Option	

9:15– 9:50

Backs—on Line and Play HB—QB—Color and Thunder (40 and 48 Auto)
Line—Rt and Lt side—Check calls and auto blocking, then by lines.
Thud plays—2 groups—Stack—Plays and 40 —48 Auto

9:50–10:15   THUD

40, 48 Auto, 43T, 45T, Scissor Rt, Lt
30 Passes
Check Out 3B, 95

10:15–10:30   Extra Points and Extra Point Defense—63 Fire

Saturday, P.M.

3:00– 3:20	Meeting— (1) Sun. Procedure
	(2) Review Punt and Punt Return
3:20– 3:25	Warm Up—A.M. Warm Up

3:25– 3:40   SPECIALTIES

Extra Points—Punt—QK
Pass and Receive
Line—Calls, Take Off

3:40– 3:50	Signals
3:50– 5:45	SCRIM—Game cond., no kick off
	45 minutes each—then in—winners go in

Monday, A.M.

NEW: 22, 23, 23C

BACKS	LINE
8:30–8:35	8:30–8:35
Warm Up	Warm Up
8:35–8:45	8:35–8:50
(1) Shuffle (2) Hit, Hit	(1) Wave (2) Balance Tackle
(3) Half Speed Tackle	(3) Boards (4) Bounce
(4) Circle Interception	Shuffle (5) Tackle Crowthers
8:45–8:55	8:50–9:15
2-on-1 Pass Defense	*Ind. Drills*
8:55–9:15	C–G: (1) Traps (2) o (8)
A and X–40 Automatic	—1 (7) Pull and Passes
Calls: 22, 23, 23–C	(3) Draws (4) 23C (25C)
B and Q–41 Power–	—23 (25)
47 Power	T: Pass Rush and Trap Re-
22, 23, 23-C–42–	action
42 Option	E: 1-on-1, 2-on-1, 40 (48)
	Auto.

9:15– 9:45 { *Backs*—
                Half Run on Lines—Add 22—23—23C
                Half Play HB—QB
     Line—Thud Plays—Add New—Check 40 Auto

9:45–10:05 { *Backs and Ends*—Roll Out Passes—40 Auto
     Line—Pass Rush and Pass Protection
          Contain QB and Tag (Jacks)

10:05–10:20 Punt and Punt Return—2 men down

10:20–10:30 { *Backs*—Ladder—Machine
     Line—Sled and Ladder

10:30–10:45 { Punt and Receive
     Kick Off   **LINE—CHALLENGE**
     Pass and Receive
     Line Auto

Monday, P.M.

4:00– 4:05	Warm Up—Agility Drills
4:05– 4:20	SPECIALTIES—Extra Points
	Pass and Receive
	Gs: 41 (47) Power—40 (48)
	Ts: Downfield Blocking Drill

BACKS	LINE

4:20–4:30
 (1) Wave   (2) Bounce
 Shuffle   (3) Down the Line
 (4) Angle Int.

4:30–4:40
 2-on-1 Pass Defense

4:40–4:55
 A and X—Pass Protection
  Calls
  40 R and P
 B and Q—40—48
  30—38
  42—42 Option
  23—22—23C

4:20–4:35
 (1) Half Speed Tackle
 (2) Hit—Hit—Hit and 2
 (3) Wave

4:35–4:55
 E: Pass Defense
 T: 1-on-1
 Gs—C: 1-on-1, 2-on-1
   63 (45) Pass Defense

4:55– 5:15 { *Backs*—Run on Lines
      Line—Review 45—54 Defense VS our Plays

5:15– 5:40

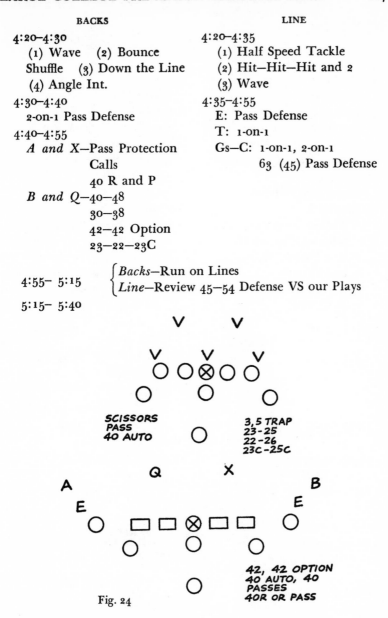

SCISSORS
PASS
40 AUTO

3,5 TRAP
23-25
22-26
23C-25C

Q   X

A   B
 E   E

42, 42 OPTION
40 AUTO, 40
PASSES
40R OR PASS

Fig. 24

5:40– 6:00	Pass Scrim
6:00– 6:10	10 Yards in
6:10– 6:15	5 and turn

Tuesday, A.M.

NEW: 63 GOAL LINE

BACKS	LINE
8:30–8:35	8:30–8:35
Warm Up	Warm Up
8:35–8:45	8:35–8:50
(1) Wave (2) Half Speed	(1) Boards (2) Wave
Tackling (3) Angle Int.	(3) Shuffle Bounce
(4) Somersault and Hit	(4) Half Speed Tackle
8:45–8:55	(5) Hit—Hit and 2
2-on-1 Pass Defense	
8:55–9:15	8:50–9:15
A and X: Calls	E: (1) 1-on-1 (2) Offside
Counter Pass Blocks	Block
Pass Protection	T: (1) 1-on-1 (2) 2-on-1
B and Q: 3 B	G-C: 3-on-3 o (8) —1 (7)
41 Power—47 Power	3 (5) Traps
42 Option	Pass and Draws

9:15– 9:40

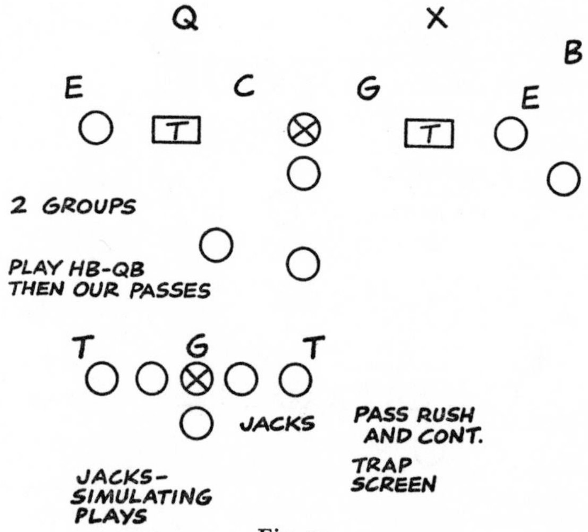

Fig. 25

9:40–10:10   THUD {Blue vs. White (Js)
                    {Red vs. Green

10:10–10:30   {*Backs*—Ladder—Gauntlet
                {*Line*—Sled—Ladder

10:30–10:45 { Pass and Pass Patterns
Punt and Receive
Kick Off

Tuesday, P.M.

4:00– 4:05   Warm up–Agility

4:05– 4:20   SPECIALTIES { Extra Points   Gs: Pulling and
Punt   Traps
Pass   Ts: Reaction
                     and HB Trap

BACKS   LINE

4:20–4:30   4:20–4:35
   (1) Shuffle   (2) Bounce   (1) Tackle Crowther
   (3) Balance Tackling   (2) Wave   (3) Bounce–Pt
   (4) Tip Drill   (4) Balance Tackle
4:30–4:40   (5) Crowther
   2 on 1 Pass Defense
4:40–4:55   4:35–4:55
   A and X   *B and Q*   E: Key Drill
   Dive Drill   Pass Protection
   Calls   23–22–25–26   (10) Int. Drills { Forward
                 40–48   BU: {   Backward
                 30–38   Tip
                                   (10) Key VS Runs
                              RGs-Ts: Rush Pass Drill
                            and Trap Reaction

4:55– 5:25

VS. MISSOURI DEFENSES

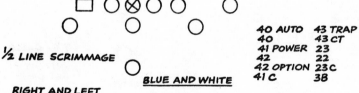

½ LINE SCRIMMAGE

40 AUTO   43 TRAP
40   43 CT
41 POWER   23
42   22
42 OPTION   23C
41 C   3B

BLUE AND WHITE

RIGHT AND LEFT
SWITCH BACKS   5:10

Fig. 26

5:25– 5:40   Goal Line Def–63
5:40– 6:05   THUD–Passes–Screens–Plays–Up and Down
                Field
6:05– 6:15   10 Yards in–Set Bags–Ts and Es–Set up and
                Man

Wednesday, A.M.

BACKS	LINE
8:30–8:35 Warm Up	8:30–8:35 Warm Up
8:35–8:45 (1) Shuffle (2) Half Speed Tackle (3)Down line (4) Balance Tackling (5) Tip	8:35–8:50 (1) Wave (2) Balance Tackle (3) Boards (4) Half-Speed Tackle
8:45–8:55 2-on-1 Pass Defense	8:50–9:15 Gs—C: 3-on-3—Keys and Assignments Ts: Def. Skills E: 1-on-1—Key Drill

8:55–9:15

A and X	B and Q
Calls	Screens

Pass Pro-
  tection
	Pass Pro-
	  tection

23—25	42—42 Option

9:15– 9:45

$$\left\{ \begin{array}{l} Backs \left\{ \begin{array}{l} \text{Half on Lines} \\ \text{Half Play HB, QB} \end{array} \right. \\[1em] Line \left\{ \begin{array}{l} \text{Half. Def. Drills (Pursuit—Splits—Rush} \\ \quad \text{Passer)} \\ \text{Half—Thud—VS our defense} \end{array} \right. \end{array} \right.$$

9:45–10:10

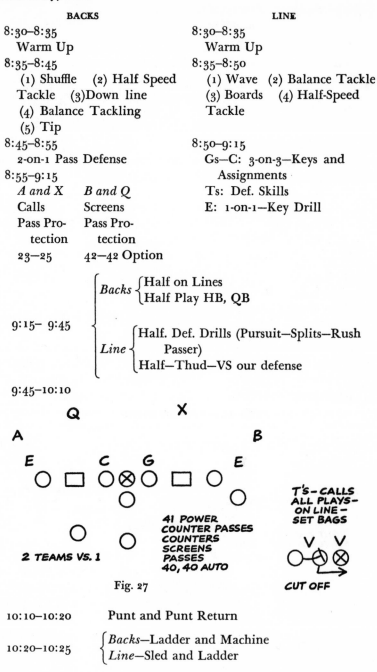

Q   X

A   B

E   C   G   E

41 POWER
COUNTER PASSES
COUNTERS
SCREENS
PASSES
40, 40 AUTO

2 TEAMS VS. 1

T'S—CALLS
ALL PLAYS—
ON LINE—
SET BAGS

CUT OFF

Fig. 27

10:10–10:20	Punt and Punt Return
10:20–10:25	Backs—Ladder and Machine Line—Sled and Ladder

10:25–10:40   SPECIALTIES $\begin{cases} \text{Pass and Receive} \\ \text{Punt and Receive} \\ \text{Kick Off} \\ \text{Extra Points} \end{cases}$

Wednesday, P.M.

3:00– 3:05   Meeting $\begin{cases} \text{All block passes—man down must go} \\ \qquad \text{to ball} \\ \text{Procedure for game} \end{cases}$

3:05– 3:10   Warm Up—By Squads
3:10– 3:20   Specialties
3:20– 3:25   Signals
3:25– 5:30   Scrim—$\begin{matrix} \text{Red vs. Green} \\ \text{Blue vs. Green and White} \end{matrix}$
7:00   Dinner

Thursday, A.M.

BACKS	LINE
8:30–8:35	8:30–8:35
Warm Up	Warm Up
8:35–8:45	8:35–8:50
(1) Wave (2) Shuffle	(1) Boards (2) Wave
(3) Bounce and Shuffle	(3) Balance Tackle
(4) Angle Interception	(4) Somersault and Hit
	(5) Hit—Hit—Hit
8:45–8:55	8:50–9:15
2-on-1	Ts: (1) Hit Shuffle and Roll
8:55–9:15	out on sled
A and X: Calls	(2) Offside cut off and
Counter Passes and	Release
Counters	(3) 1-on-1
30–60 Lanes	Es: (1) 2-on-1 (2) 1-on-1
B and Q: 41 Power—41C	G-C: (1) Shuffle—Hit Sled
30–38	(2) lock man inside
40–48	(3) 47C (41C) Pass
Screens	

9:15– 9:35 $\begin{cases} \textit{Backs}\text{—Flood Drill} \\ \textit{Line}\text{—Thud VS our defenses} \end{cases}$

Thursday, A.M.

9:35– 9:55	{ *Backs and Ends*	1 Set—Drop back with Es Rush 2 Sets—Roll Out passes VS Es
	Line—Pass Protection and Screens—Draw	

9:55–10:25   THUD—Half Line VS Eagle and Over shift 5-3
                  and Tight State
                  (Js—with left side)

10:25–10:30   { *Backs*—Ladder and Machine
                    Line—Sled and Ladder

10:30–10:45   SPECIALTIES

Thursday, P.M.

4:00– 4:05   Warm Up—Agility

4:05– 4:20   SPECIALTIES   { Ts—HB and Gd Trap Reaction
                               Gds—o-1 Pull

BACKS	LINE
4:20–4:30	4:20–4:35
(1) Shuffle (2) Hit, Hit	(1) Bounce Shuffle (2) Wave
(3) Half Speed Tackle	(3) Boards (4) Half Speed
(4) Circle Interception	Tackle
4:30–4:40	4:35–4:55
2 on 1	RG—Ts: Rush Passer
4:40–4:55	Es: 54 Key VS Flanker
A and X: Dive Drill	BUs: (1) Key 63 Def.—
Spread Double Team	Passes
Tackle and End	(2) Key 54 Def.—
B and Q: 42	Passes and Run
23—22	
Pass Prot.	

4:55– 5:15   { *Backs* { Half Play HB, QB
                                  { Half on Line
                    Line—Thud VS over shift 5-3

5:15– 5:55   Pass Scrim—Off and Def—Tag—2 on 1
5:55– 6:05   Punt and Punt Return
6:05– 6:15   Signals—10 yards in.

Friday, A.M.

NEW: KICK OFF RETURN

BACKS	LINE

8:30–8:35
 Warm Up

8:35–8:45
 (1) Shuffle   (2) Circle
 Interception   (3) Balance
 Tackle   (4) Half Speed
 Tackling

8:45–8:55
 2-on-1 Pass Defense

8:55–9:15
 A and X: Boards
   40 R or P
 B and Q: 42
   23
   41 Power

8:30–8:35
 Warm Up

8:35–8:50
 (1) Boards   (2) Hit–Hit
 (3) Bounce Shuffle   (4) Wave

8:50–9:15
 Es: Calls, Releases, Cts, Traps
 Ts: Defense (Del. Blow–Trap
   Pursuit)
 G-C: (1) 1-on-1, 2-on-1
   (2) Bal. Pass Prot.
   (3) Draw

9:15– 9:45
Pass Off. and Def.

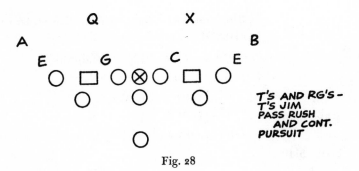

T'S AND RG'S—
T'S JIM
PASS RUSH
   AND CONT.
   PURSUIT

Fig. 28

9:45– 9:55   Punt and Punt Return—4 men down
      (Js)

9:55–10:20   Rt and left side—Thud VS 62—over shift 5-3—
      State

10:20–10:30   { *Backs*—Ladder and Machine
        { *Line*—Sled—Ladder

Friday, A.M.

10:30–10:45   SPECIALTIES $\begin{cases}\text{Pass and Pass Patterns}\\\text{Extra Pts. and Kick off}\\\text{Punt and Receive}\\\text{Challenge}\end{cases}$

Friday, P.M.

4:00– 4:05   Warm Up–Agility
4:05– 4:20   SPECIALTIES

BACKS   LINE

4:20–4:30   4:20–4:30
  Dive Gauntlet Drill   *Ind. Drills*

E: $\bigr\}$ 45 Key
T:

G-C: $\begin{cases}63\\54\end{cases}$ Gap–Keys

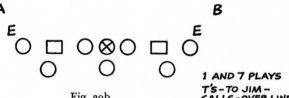

Fig. 29a

4:30– 4:55 $\begin{cases}\text{Blue and Red–Thud–Screens, Passes, Draws}\\\text{MISSOURI plays–VS our defenses–}\end{cases}$

$\begin{cases}\text{MO–Green backs–White line}\\\quad\text{Green–Line on def}\end{cases}$

4:55– 5:20 $\begin{cases}Backs\begin{cases}\text{Half play HB–QB}\\\text{Half on line}\end{cases}\\Line\text{–7 on 7 and Stack}\end{cases}$

5:20– 5:40

A   B

E   E

1 AND 7 PLAYS
T'S - TO JIM -
CALLS - OVER LINE

Fig. 29b

5:40– 6:00   Kick off and Kick off return–4
6:00– 6:10   Signals–10 yards in
6:10– 6:15   Grass Drill

Saturday, A.M.

BACKS	LINE
8:35–8:40 Warm Up	8:35–8:40 Warm Up
8:40–8:55 Corner–Drill for A and B	8:40–8:55 Gs and C–3 on 3
8:55–9:15 Run on Lines–½ Es Key Backs	Es–Everyday Drills Ts–Sled–Roll Outs and Shuffle
	8:55–9:15 ½ Es and Interior Line Def VS MO Offense

9:15– 9:35 $\begin{cases} \textit{Backs and Es–}\text{No Defense–Run all pass lanes} \\ \textit{Int. Line–}\text{Screens–40 Auto–43 Trap–Counters} \end{cases}$

9:35–10:00

RED AND BLUE–1 AND 7–0–8–PASSES

T'S – JIM CALLS ON LINE PASS RUSH AND DEF. – 1 ON 1 – ½ E'S – PURSUIT

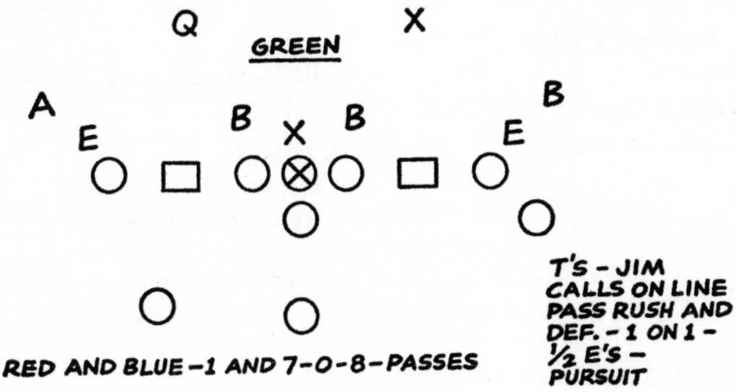

Fig. 30

10:00–10:25	THUD–upfield–Blue VS Red– (Joe–Tor–Jim) Stationary–Green VS White–Shift individuals (Pat, Dan, and J. T.)
10:25–10:30	*Backs*–Side line drill *Line*–Sled
10:30–10:40	SPECIALTIES

Saturday, P.M.

3:00– 3:10 Meeting $\begin{cases} \text{Pre-Game warm up} \\ \text{Mistakes} \end{cases}$

Saturday, P.M.

3:10– 3:18	Punters and Cs—Out—Warm Up and Punt
3:13– 3:18	Line out—Warm Up and Starts—by 1 QB

3:18– 3:23 $\left\{\begin{array}{l}\text{Kick Off}\\ \text{Backs and Es—Pass and Receive}\\ \text{1 QB—at Extra Points}\end{array}\right.$

3:23– 3:25	Signals by teams
3:25– 5:40	Scrim—1 VS 2

Monday, A.M.

9:30– 9:40   Warm Up and Agility
              (Shuffle—Wave—Balance Tackle)

BACKS	LINE
9:40–9:50	9:40–9:55
Interception, Shuffle, Wave, Balance Tackle	Wave—Balance Tackle and Sled
9:50–10:10	BUs—Shuffle and Interception Drill
Run on lines and C Passes 1 team on Def. Key	9:55–10:10
	Pursuit Drill on Sled BUs—Reactions

10:10–10:25 $\left\{\begin{array}{l}\textit{Line and Half Es} \text{ VS MO Offense}\\ \textit{Backs}\text{—Pass Patterns and Half Es}\end{array}\right.$

10:25–10:35	Punt Return
10:35–10:45	Signals and Sprints

Monday, P.M.

NEW: *Goal Line—54 Blow*

SPECIALTIES

3:30– 3:35   Warm Up—Agility

3:35– 3:50 $\left\{\begin{array}{l}\text{Es—Key Short side HB}\\ \text{BUs—Key Drill}\\ \text{Backs—Run on lines—Dive Drill}\\ \text{Ts—RGs—Boards—Sled—Fire}\end{array}\right.$

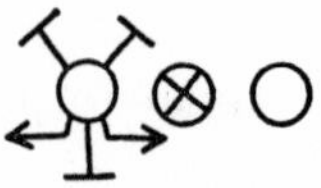

Fig. 31a

Backs $\left\{\begin{array}{l}\text{2 on 1 Pass Def (A1)}\\ \text{Flood Drill}\end{array}\right.$

3:50– 4:05

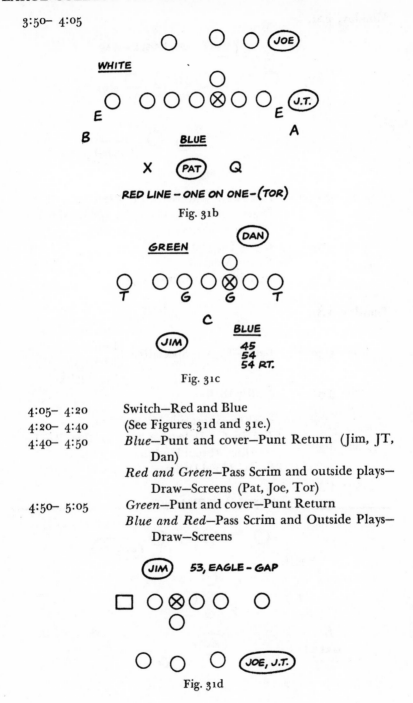

WHITE

E

B   BLUE   A

X   PAT   Q

RED LINE – ONE ON ONE–(TOR)

Fig. 31b

GREEN   DAN

T   G   G   T

C   BLUE

JIM   45
54
54 RT.

Fig. 31c

4:05– 4:20	Switch–Red and Blue
4:20– 4:40	(See Figures 31d and 31e.)
4:40– 4:50	*Blue*–Punt and cover–Punt Return (Jim, JT, Dan)
	Red and Green–Pass Scrim and outside plays– Draw–Screens (Pat, Joe, Tor)
4:50– 5:05	*Green*–Punt and cover–Punt Return
	Blue and Red–Pass Scrim and Outside Plays– Draw–Screens

JIM   53, EAGLE – GAP

JOE, J.T.

Fig. 31d

Monday, P.M.

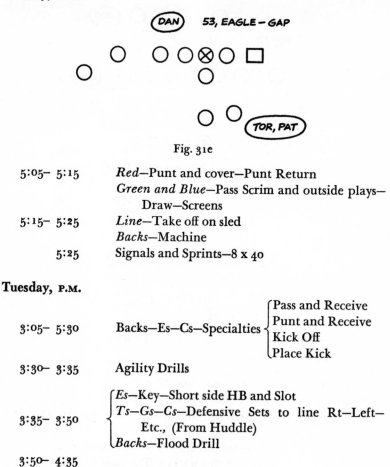

Fig. 31e

5:05– 5:15	*Red*—Punt and cover—Punt Return
	Green and Blue—Pass Scrim and outside plays— Draw—Screens
5:15– 5:25	*Line*—Take off on sled
	Backs—Machine
5:25	Signals and Sprints—8 x 40

Tuesday, P.M.

3:05– 5:30	Backs—Es—Cs—Specialties $\begin{cases} \text{Pass and Receive} \\ \text{Punt and Receive} \\ \text{Kick Off} \\ \text{Place Kick} \end{cases}$
3:30– 3:35	Agility Drills
3:35– 3:50	$\begin{cases} Es\text{—Key—Short side HB and Slot} \\ Ts\text{—}Gs\text{—}Cs\text{—Defensive Sets to line Rt—Left—} \\ \quad \text{Etc., (From Huddle)} \\ Backs\text{—Flood Drill} \end{cases}$
3:50– 4:35	

PASSES AND ROLL-OUTS

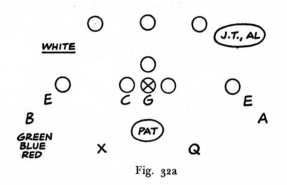

Fig. 32a

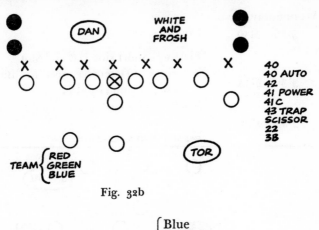

Fig. 32b

Cs—Backs on Line $\begin{cases} \text{Blue} \\ \text{Red} \\ \text{Green} \end{cases}$

Ts—RG — Line—no C
Green	Blue	$\begin{cases} \text{Pass Rush and Contain} \\ \text{Pursuit (Jim)} \\ \text{Shifting Defenses} \end{cases}$
Blue	Red	
Red	Green	

4:35– 4:50 $\begin{cases} \textit{Red}\text{—Def VS Missouri} \\ \textit{Blue and Green}\text{—Pass off VS 5—6—7 man rush} \\ \quad \text{(MO team if possible)} \\ \quad \text{(40 auto—Screens—Draw)} \end{cases}$

4:50– 5:05 $\begin{cases} \textit{Green}\text{—Def VS MO} \\ \textit{Blue and Red}\text{—Pass Off} \end{cases}$

5:05– 5:20 $\begin{cases} \textit{Blue}\text{—Def VS MO} \\ \textit{Red and Green}\text{—Pass Off} \end{cases}$

5:20– 5:25 $\begin{cases} \textit{Line}\text{—Sled} \\ \textit{Backs}\text{—Machine} \end{cases}$

5:25– 5:30   Signals from a spot—Condition

7:30   Meeting

Wednesday, P.M.

3:05– 3:30   Backs—Es—Cs—Specialties $\begin{cases} \text{Pass and Receive} \\ \text{Punt and Receive} \\ \text{Kick Off} \\ \text{Place Kick} \end{cases}$

Wednesday, P.M.

    3:25– 3:30   Line—

    3:30– 3:45 $\begin{cases} Es\text{—Key—Short side HB and Slot} \\ Ts\text{—}Gs\text{—}Cs\text{—Defensive Sets to line Rt—Left—} \\ \quad\text{etc., (From Huddle)} \\ Backs\text{—Flood Drill} \end{cases}$

    3:45– 4:30

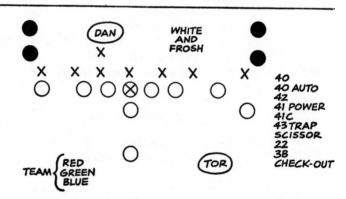

PASSES AND ROLL-OUTS

Fig. 33

Cs—Backs on Line $\begin{cases} \text{Blue} \\ \text{Red} \\ \text{Green} \end{cases}$
    (Joe)

Ts—Rg—Line—no C $\begin{cases} \text{Pass Rush and Contain} \\ \text{Pursuit (Jim)} \\ \text{Shifting Defenses} \\ \text{Ext. VS Slot} \\ 54 \text{ R.L.—}45 \end{cases}$

Green   Blue
Blue   Red
Red   Green

4:30– 4:45	*Green*–Def VS Missouri–54 R and L–45–54–
	    Goal Line
	Blue and Red–Punt–8 Man Rush–then Pass
	    Off (40 Auto–Screens–Draw)

4:45– 5:00	*Red*–Def vs MO *Blue and Green*–Pass Off
5:00– 5:15	*Blue*–Def vs MO *Red and Green*–Pass Off
5:15– 5:20	*Line*–Sled *Backs*–Machine
5:20– 5:30	Punt and Punt Return
7:30	Meeting–Report
10:00	Meeting at Stadium

MO Team Run

Quick Kick
Sally
Single Wing
Deep Single Wing
Motion–Off Tackle Play
46 and Passes

Thursday, P.M.

3:00– 3:20	Es–Backs–Cs–Warm Up and Specialties
3:15– 3:20	Line–Warm Up
3:20– 3:30	*Green and Blue*–Kick Off and Receive–Field Goal and 63 Fire–Def. *Red*–Thud VS White–MO Defenses
3:30– 3:40	*Blue and Red*–Kick Off and Receive–Field Goal and 63 Fire–Def. *Green*–Thud–VS White
3:40– 3:50	*Red and Green*–Kick Off and Receive–Field Goal and 63 Fire–Def. *Blue*–Thud–VS White–MO Defenses
3:50– 4:05	*Green*–Defenses and Punt Return–VS White *Blue and Red*–Pass and Thud

Thursday, P.M.

4:05– 4:20   { *Red*—Defenses and Punt Return VS White MO
                  { *Green and Blue*—Pass Offense and Thud

4:20– 4:35   { *Blue*—Defenses and Punt Return—VS White
                       MO
                  { *Red and Green*—Pass Off and Thud

4:35– 4:45   Signals—Hold Points

SUMMARY

Chapter 8 presented two major college pre-season practice schedules as an example of content, continuity of detail, organization, and methods of coaching. The Air Force program is limited to the first week only to provide a larger sampling for your evaluation while the Penn State practice plan is complete until its opening game. Both programs show detail of ultimate organization. Larger and more skillful player personnel painstakingly selected through the most rigorous competition demands that the major college staff be well versed in its functions. Practice calls for more specialized individual work which extends cohesively into complete team integration. The work progresses from the movie-chalk session to the field and back to the blackboard for additional chalk sessions. The head coach must be a master-organizer and his delegation of duties to his staff can determine the success of his whole program. The work is enormous in planning and executing which quite often may cover sixteen hours a day. The job calls for the ultimate in planning and the responsibility is so great that pressure of varying standards underlies the whole staff which in turn makes each coach willing to dedicate his personal efforts to the success of the program. The practice plans presented in this chapter can offer many ideas to coaches from the junior high school to the small college and even other major college mentors.

9

PROGRAM FOR THE SPECIALIST

Every Player Is a Specialist

In the minds of the average layman, and even to a degree in the minds of many coaches, a football player possessing punting, kicking-off, and point after touchdown abilities is a specialist. This is true, but the word specialist covers every player on the squad. Each player is a specialist in his own position and must master certain skills for that position. For example, guards and tackles are not considered specialists in a true sense of the word, yet they are specialists in the art of blocking and tackling, and, therefore, are required to practice certain skills which will make them more proficient in carrying out the functions of their positions. Pulling out of the line to lead a play by a running guard or tackle must be learned and perfected by practice. A few minutes daily can suffice in the mastery of such a skill and pay off dividends in offensive excellence. Because every player is a specialist in his own right should make some form of program mandatory in the improvement of these talents. Some form of practice program must be planned to insure meeting the needs of the specialists. The program will vary with the specialist and the type of talent he possesses; some will need more practice than others. Keep in mind that a limited program is better than no program at all.

Time and Place in the Daily Program

Your practice time allotment and your own school program will determine whether you place the work of the specialist at the beginning of practice or at the end and will also limit the time available. In many schools today involving jointures bus schedules create a scheduling problem as does dining hall regulations in many small colleges. Coaches involved in jointures set up noon hour programs for their specialists. Many hold formal practice during the noon hour which is coupled with an activity period prominent in many schools and keep certain specialists out after school or have them released from study periods expressedly set up for this purpose. Some coaches prefer having their specialists practice before formal practice begins basing their reasons on the fact that the majority of the squad will be on the practice field several minutes before the start of formal practice. Some boys are naturally slow dressers while others need equipment changes or taping and minor medical care. Rather than having the squad milling around on the field, gathered in social groups, or practicing skills they will never be called upon to use; the coach has his assistants execute a specialists program. Normally such a period covers at least fifteen minutes which is sufficiently long for even the most demanding specialist. A specialist program prior to formal practice does have merit in that it can keep all players positively active and allows for teaching certain skills to boys inexperienced or lacking in some qualities. The specialist program conducted after practice usually involves only the most-skilled and those possessing the essential specialities such as punting, passing, safety men, kick-off and point after touchdown experts. It normally involves from one-third to one-half of the squad personnel.

This book recommends a combination of before and after practice specialists program. Guards, tackles, ends, and linebackers can complete their specialities before formal practice begins and not be required to remain after practice. Since backs must be more proficient in their skills and do have more to master than linemen, they should be required to remain after practice along with the boys possessing those extra skills which

may decide the outcome of any given game, namely: the punters, kick-off, place kickers, centers, safety men, and quarterbacks.
These boys should practice warm-up and fundamental drills in
the pre-practice period or join in on other drills suitable to
their position.

Program for the Guards and Tackles

Since the functions of the guards and tackles are somewhat
similar and dependent upon each other the drills can encompass both positions. They should cover brief warm up calisthenics for limbering purposes, pulling-out, cross-blocking,
quick charges, and machine work. Drills employing two or more
of these basic skills are to be recommended. Jim Bonder, head
coach at West Chester State College, Pennsylvania, used a short
three minute drill that covered blocking, tackling, and reaction
which each player performed as soon as he hit the field. The
drill, of course, is dependent upon having all of your linemen
present at a certain time. A minimum of five pull-outs to each
side with rounding of the corner and sprinting to a would-be
tackler of at least five-yards distance is recommended. At least
five crossblocks should be executed along with an equal number
of stance charges for improving speed. Five tackles on each
shoulder against the machine should be a minimum requirement. Two lunge blocks on each shoulder; three shoulder
blocks on each shoulder; three cross body blocks on each hip;
five shiv thrusts on the middle bar of the charger-blocker machine plus three head pushes on the same bar should constitute
basic requirements offensively and defensively on the machine.

A Recommended Pre-Practice Drill for Guards and Tackles

Consult the field chart at the close of this chapter and try to
visualize the progress of the following recommended drill for
guards and tackles which can be executed under a coach's direction or unsupervised. The discipline of your squad will determine the effectiveness of unsupervised pre-practice speciality
drill. The men in question congregate at a designated area and
limber themselves up with some snappy calisthenics for about
two minutes. They then form a straight forward line. One man

acts as a signal caller. Alternate linemen pull left or right as directed while the in-between linemen charge forward. There is a rotation of the whole process so that every player pulls and charges. This drill will satisfy the recommended five pull-outs to each side and cover the stance charges for speed improvement.

Next, a quick romp through the tires (at least 10 pair) for leg agility. The tire drill is followed by the board drill in which a player holds a dummy at the front of the board. In succession each guard and tackle drives the dummy, with the holder offering moderate resistance, to the rear with choppy, driving steps spread the width of the 14-inch board. Players alternate holding the bags.

As they clear the boards, the first six to eight men grab an air dummy or a light (22 pound) bag. In alternating-successive interchange each man completes a cross body and shoulder block followed by a tackle. They repeat the procedure according to the number of bags and dummies or can go around twice. From this drill they go on to the two man charger-blocker sled where additional blocks and tackles can be added in addition to fulfilling lunge blocks (belly-slammers), shiv tactics and neck pushes.

All of the recommended activities, if actively and spiritedly performed, should consume about ten minutes. Your guards and tackles will have covered their specialities and will be ready for advanced work. It may be noted that the board drill is also recommended for the centers and ends. They can execute the requirements between themselves.

Ends

Ends should practice footwork daily. Most people have a misconstrued notion that ends are primarily pass receivers. Ends probably have more functions to perform and the most skills to learn than any position on a football team. They not only have more than a few defensive responsibilities on the line, but must also afford pass defense requirements, rush punters, cover punts, limit the offense to the central portion of the playing field, receive passes, carry the ball on end around plays, plus shovel passes, and possess more endurance than any player on the field.

End Shuffle Drill

All ends should execute a short shuffle drill as soon as they are warmed up. One end can be the would-be passer-runner while two ends take their defensive position.* If the runner comes forward the ends converge upon him; if he retreats both ends drop back quickly; if he goes to one side that end drifts with him to the sideline while the other end follows cautiously. Should the ball carrier reverse to the other side the drifting end pursues cautiously while the pursuing end becomes the drifter. The ball carrier should mix up his tactics and set a fast pace for a full minute which will have all three boys gasping for a rest. (See Field Chart)

End Feint Drill

Each end should practice every feint he has been taught at least twice to rid himself of a defender or get that necessary one step advantage for a successful pass completion. As shown on the chart, they should line up in two lines, then execute under supervision of a coach, a manager, or another end (who will take his turn also) the following points: change of pace (slow then burst of speed); down ten and hook back one step; ten steps and hook both in and out; ten and hook and go deep, five to seven and angle sharply to sidelines; deep with speed (bomb); banana; two and out sharp; look-in; wait; and finally the quickie.

One-Handed Receiving Drill

Ends should pair off by twos and play a one-handed catch game for about two minutes. Such a drill teaches finger control. It also strengthens the fingers and wrists and makes two-handed ball catching much easier. Both paired ends face each other about eight yards apart. One tosses the ball so that the other must stretch his full length with arm up-raised or leave

* Diagrammed in the November 1959, issue of *Athletic Journal*, "Notebook of Defensive Drills," by G. A. Katchmer.

his feet to contact the ball. He must try to grasp it with his extended hand for a completed catch. He should not knock it down then catch it. Both arms should be alternated and the thrown pass soft, yet moderate. The ends toss back and forth to each other. They should finish up the drill with a few running one handed catches which teaches them to hook the ball into the receiving hand.

Goal Post Drill

It might be added that the following goal post drill should precede all of the other end drills. This drill is to teach steps, reaction, and drift. In lines on each side of the upright goal bars, the first end in each line positions himself one step to the outside. On a signal, he steps with the outside foot first, then the inside foot and makes shiv contact with the post followed by the outside foot either forward to seal off the inside or be ready to drift and drop back (in case of pass coverage). Crashing by the posts to a given spot can also be practiced in simulating rushing the passer.

Pass Drills

If time permits, the ends can join the backs for pass receiving drills. Otherwise, these drills must be practiced after practice. Each feint or pass pattern cut practiced earlier should be executed in these drills. The drills are recommended for after practice due to the allotment of time required. At least fifteen minutes are prescribed and snappy execution is demanded if the drills are to be completed.

Centers

Centers, because of necessity, must be a part of speciality drills before and after practice. They should be required to work for more proficiency on their snap-backs prior to formal practice. Centers can pair off with each other immediately after warming up and practice a minimum of 10 snap-backs to a T-quarterback; 10 to a single wing tailback with leads to either side; five to the single wing fullback snapping to left and right sides; and 10 to a punt formation punter at a minimum of 15 yards.

Weighted balls are available today which helps build wrist and forearm strength. Centers can warm up with them in these drills. In addition to snapping drills, the centers should practice about five fast drop-backs looking right or left to see if a prospective receiver is crossing in front in which case they would be ready to jam him then continue back to the hook spot for pass defense.

After completion of these pre-practice drills the centers should make themselves available to backs, passers, and punters.

Linebackers

Guards, centers, and fullbacks who double as linebackers should practice about two minutes daily prior to practice coming across fast three, four, or five steps to meet an outside run or stunting to a certain spot from a supposed middle linebacking spot. They should also practice from five to ten drop-backs to the hook spot and then fan to the sidelines for pass coverage. These drills can be executed independently while in line for other drills. They can also be combined with the deep secondary. A coach should supervise this drill.

Deep Secondary

All backs should spend at least two minutes daily on some form of rotating drill against the roll-out, pitch-out, or belly series. A good drill to recommend is the one used by the ends. As the runner sweeps outside the secondary rotates to the ball; if he drops the secondary drop into zone pass positions; and if he comes forward the backs converge upon him.

Kick-Off Platoon

An assistant coach should gather the kick-off squad for two kick-offs daily and time the first and last man to reach the receiver who does not attempt to run back the ball. This drill will teach the men to speed to the receiver and not jockey around with would-be blockers. The drill makes speed habitual. Quite often a coach will be seen tearing his hair because his team loafed getting down under a kick-off or were jockeying with blockers at the expense of valuable yardage return.

Quarterbacks

Quarterbacks should warm up then limber their arms like any baseball pitcher. They should pass to one another aiming the ball at different spots, namely: right shoulder, left shoulder, right arm extended, left arm extended, over the head, at the chest, and into the stomach. They should execute the down-on-one knee passing drill and also practice dropping back to the passing pocket with all speed. They should spend at least two to three minutes on lateral passes, shovel pass, and the pitch-out pass. After these individual skill drills the quarterbacks should take over the passing lanes and throw at least one of every type pass they must perform in a game such as the jump or quickie pass, short bullet pass, lob pass, the lead pass to the sidelines, the hook man, the long pass, roll-out pass, the look in pass, and a pass to a stationary receiver such as a lonely end or split receiver. If they possess other specialities such as punting, place kicking, etc. they must put forth the extra practice during the main specialists session.

Post-Practice Specialists Session

Punters, safety men, quick-kickers, place kickers, holders, passers, receivers, and centers are normally the specialists in a true sense of the word. Since they must perform under game pressure the fatigue produced by the practice session will be a more valid criterion of how they will perform during a game. Performing their specialities after an hour or more of practice can tell you the reserve stamina they still possess to carry out their specialities to desired efficiency Of course, passers and receivers in many instances may have plenty of time available in the pre-practice session which would not require them to remain after practice.

Punters

There will be no attempt here to teach the fine art of punting. However, the author recommends very highly Don Fuoss' book, *The Complete Kicking Game* (Prentice-Hall, Inc., Englewood Cliffs, New Jersey, 1959). The material covered will attempt to suggest a practice routine for improving kicking skills and maintaining peak efficiency.

The punter like the passer and baseball pitcher must limber up his leg with a few leg stretching and leg-lift drills followed by some shadow kicking. This despite a full practice session already completed. Kicking involves the leg muscles in other forms of exertion than running, etc. A few warm-up kicks at medium strength and the punter should be ready for his kicking chores.

Time Limit or Number of Punts Prescribed

Some coaches feel that the punter should punt at least 15 minutes while others advocate 10, 15, or 20 punts. The author does not believe in any specified attempts or a time limit but rather feels that the punter should determine his need. A list of punts should be specified for practice such as out-of-bounds kicking, straight down the middle for distance and high down the middle for punts from the 50 to 35 yard lines. Steps should be checked and also speed in getting off the kicks. The punter should be timed to insure getting off his kick in less than two seconds with the goal set at 1.6 seconds. The punter should practice the different punts until he feels a certain satisfaction that he has reached his peak of efficiency. Once he begins to feel tired and his kicks start to lose distance he has reached his physiological limit, then it is time to go for his shower. There will be days when he may not reach his peak of efficiency, and, under such circumstances, it is recommended that 15 minutes should be his maximum practice time. On days when he is in prime punting form time can be varied from five to ten minutes. Allow the punter to gauge his own needs and efficiency.

Caution Should Be Observed in Punting Drills

A note of caution to keep in mind is the size and strength of your punter. Legs like pitching arms can be strained. As a result, some coaches do not allow their punters to practice punting the day before a game. Size in itself is not a deterrent to punting ability. My punter last fall, Steve Bednar, a 145 pound 5'8" freshman, pulled us out of many a tight hole and put opponents in several situations that led to touchdowns for us with punts that traveled 50 to 60 yards in the air.

Another caution to observe is over-coaching. Don't change the natural style of your punter as long as he is getting distance on his punts. Back in my college playing days at Lebanon Valley College, Eddie Kress did all of our punting. He had the most unorthodox method of holding and dropping the ball from a north-south position that few punters would be able to get any distance and definitely no spiral yet Ed seldom got off a poor punt and ranked with the best in statistics. My punter, Steve Bednar, was a one-hand drop punter yet performance is the criterion.

Another caution to practice is to limit the number punting. Pick out your good ones and see that they practice unhindered. Take any boys interested in learning the techniques of punting and put them in a group by themselves. Delegate a coach to the group for instructing purposes.

Safety Men

Safety men should practice five receptions, namely: (1) fair catch; (2) taking the ball on the dead run; (3) playing in close and going back for the ball; (4) going to the right side; (5) going to the left side catching the ball on the run; and possibly a sixth reception, i.e., playing the bounding ball.

Double safeties can practice the reverse handoff used with Daisy Chain blocking. Remember, the man handing off the ball must be in front of the receiver. The ball should be covered with both arms and slid out with the front arm into a pocket formed by the receiver who lifts his inside elbow and takes the ball with the palm of his outside hand while the raised elbow clamps down to close the pocket and hide the ball.

Quick Kicker

The quick kicker should warm up similar to the punter. On the drop back type of quick-kicker speed in dropping and distance are requisites along with minimum of steps in kicking and speed of punting the ball. These take practice and the kicker should be timed to reach a maximum of speed goal. The kicker must drop at least three steps and try to punt the ball on one step. Washington, D. C. Teachers had a big fullback who could perform from a rock-step after dropping three steps, getting off quick-kicks that traveled 50 or more yards in the air. It takes practice. Quite often a boy who is very inefficient as a punter makes a good quick-kicker. The main purpose is to get the ball away with sufficient height to clear the secondary but with enough power to generate a goalward bounding ball. A spiraled kick is not necessary.

The quick-kicking halfback who kicks from a side step must practice the proper step along with a swinging motion of his kicking foot. Again, because of his proximity to the line of scrimmage, speed is a prerequisite in getting off the kick.

The prescribed dosage of practice is recommended in line with the punters. Let the kicker pace himself and determine his performance peak.

Kick-Off Men

As for the other kickers a warm-up period is necessary. Distance kick-offs are desired and the kickers should practice trying to kick the ball into the end zone thus eliminating the return. Some coaches prefer a flat kick, because it has the unpredictability of the knuckle ball in baseball. It may sail and dip and its bounce is hard to gauge. Both types of kick-offs should be practiced. A certain amount of kicks can be prescribed, however, it is felt that a kicker reaches a certain peak in distance and then begins to decline. This could happen in five, ten, or fifteen minute periods. When the peak of performance begins to decline no amount of practice will show improvement; thus it is time to call it a day.

P.A.T. and Place Kickers

These specialists should follow the same requirements and limitations followed by the other kickers. For the point-after-touchdown specialist steps, speed, eye on the ball spot, follow through, and accuracy are the skills to master.

The place-kickers must master the same fundamentals but from greater distances and different angles. Practice is very

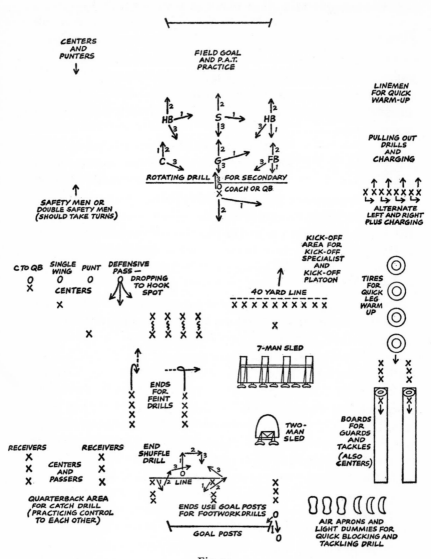

Fig. 34

essential in improving this speciality. Both specialists should simulate game conditions as much as possible.

Holder

These men need practice in catching the ball and speed in placing it at the proper angle which means they must know the different kickers and their preference of ball slant. They must also maintain a good body balance and be ready to spring into action in case of a blocked kick.

Off-Season or Summer Practice

Many coaches today require their specialists to undergo weight training during the off-season. Others have netting constructed for their kickers while still others use the field house for certain prescribed activities. Specialists should be given the proper equipment such as balls, shoes, etc. to practice their specialities. The same dosage outlined in this chapter which normally would cover five to fifteen minutes daily is recommended with the advocacy of rope skipping for all personnel to improve agility.

SUMMARY

The chapter, "Program for the Specialist," may be somewhat lacking in detail for the various specialities and perhaps omit some few; however, in a book of such magnitude where geographical sampling is stretched as much as possible to include as many programs as possible, a certain limitation must be exercised. Specialized work, in itself, can cover a volume. The author assumes that the majority of coaches are familiar with the details for the specialist, and, therefore, recommends a program based upon amount, time, and place in the over-all program. The chapter just completed has tried to impress the reader that some type of program must be prescribed for every player since it is assumed that every squad member is a specialist to a degree. Such programs are recommended both before and after practice. The program before practice will satisfy the requirements for the majority of the players and keep them actively occupied until formal practice begins; while the post-practice specialist program will test the major specialist under as near game duress as possible. A program is prescribed for every player either under coaching supervision or under player team discipline with a field chart locating each activity. Time allotments, number of performances, and before or after practice execution is recommended in the chapter. There may be coaching disagreements with the material, but the sampling enclosed is based upon many coaching philosophies.

10

OFF-FIELD ACTIVITIES

Activities Many and Varied

The work carried on by the coach and his staff away from the field of practice are so varied and many that any given one could seriously impede the progress being achieved in the daily work-outs. Each contributes an integral part to the overall football framework; thus necessitating complete fidelity to organization and detail. This chapter will endeavor to cover 19 of these activities with the realization that the list is not complete, but these are the most essential.

Managers

A good manager is a blessing in disguise and his value to a coach is immeasurable. A staff of three or more good managers can be considered a gift from Santa Claus. They are as valuable to a head coach as his staff in alleviating him of countless chores. Good managers do not just happen; they must be selected and trained. Lazy, indolent, boys do not qualify nor does the comedian type although the latter often pays up for laxity in boosting team morale. Quite often boys sign up as managers only to become the executive type, that is, managers in name only. The coach must carefully prepare a check list of managerial duties and break them down to specific boys such as one boy responsible for laundry, towels, etc.; another for equipment; one or two for practice field duties; and other chores according to the number of boys available. The size of the managerial staff should not carry any definite limitations, because boys are becoming more and more loath to accept the work and responsibility involved by the position. All managers should be placed under the supervision of a senior manager. The training of this senior manager may entail many painstaking hours on the part of the coach, but, once trained, this boy can train others as they come up the echelon. In many colleges the senior manager is paid a seasonal fee. The managerial problem is an acute one in many small colleges, because the awarding of a letter has lost its significance in comparison to the work involved.

Faculty Equipment Manager

It is recommended that the coach secure the services of a faculty member, if at all possible, to assume the duties of equipment manager. The theft of equipment can reach expensive proportions and is difficult to control without proper storage space and definite checking. Actually school administrators do not realize that, even by paying such a faculty-equipment man, the savings prevented in thievery of jerseys, etc. will more than pay this salary over a period of time. A good equipment manager can add years to playing material through repair, cleaning, proper fit, and good storage. The coach who must handle this chore along with his other duties has a man-sized job which he must delegate to student managers and supervise very closely. It would not be difficult to get a faculty representative, even in a small high school, for a token fee of $50 to $100.

Trainer

In a similar vein wherever possible an adult should be entrusted with the responsibilities of trainer. Oftentimes a faculty member can be talked into such a position. A sympathetic administration or school board can be influenced in such a way as to dole out a small fee for the services rendered. Many laymen, especially recent alumni, will volunteer their services when properly approached. Should these people be unavailable then the coach and his staff naturally find themselves burdened with this additional function. This necessitates the training of one or more student trainers which becomes a tiresome chore year after year yet one that can render a great return in economy of time for the coach. The coach must insist on the players helping themselves as much as possible after a period of orientation and practice in handling minor injuries and ankle-wrapping. Boys should be taught to work in pairs especially in applying the figure eight or Louisiana type ankle-wrap.

Training Room Rules

A set of training room rules must be exhibited and brought to the team's attention. Boys must be impressed with the importance of the training room personnel and asked to show every consideration in their demands upon the trainers. Unexcused last minute rushes for tape jobs, the desire for pampering and attention, and the hypochondriac type boy must be strictly controlled. Again it points to establishing set procedures and off-field activity organization from the coach.

The Chalk Session

As an off-field activity, and one so closely associated with the actual work on the field, the chalk session or talk must be as minutely planned as the practice sessions. The two go hand in hand since the chalk talk explains by words, diagram, or picture the work undertaken on the field or to be experienced during practice. It is an orientation period used for teaching and emphasis. The manual becomes a vital part of these sessions since it is the basic text and contains the information, charts and diagrams that constitute the football program being taught.

Meetings should be short, direct and to the point while covering the essential material. Long-winded harangues or long pep talks have no place in the chalk session. As the head man have your material ready to present; present it without losing the attention of your boys or putting a few of them to sleep. Don't try to cover more material than the experience of your boys will allow them to absorb. Chalk talks should not be held for the sake of having a meeting, but a well directed session will alleviate your field chores. Keep in mind that any chalk session is a good one when the boys ask questions.

High School Chalk Sessions

On the high school level chalk sessions should be kept to a maximum of one hour in order to keep the attention of your boys. Their frequency must depend upon the time of season, time available, and experience of the squad. During the pre-season practice schedule a suitable meeting time is no problem, because the period between morning and afternoon sessions is the most logical time. A fifteen minute orientation period before morning practice can also be productive from a practice time-economy standpoint.

Once school commences a suitable meeting time may become a problem due to local school conditions such as jointures, union schools, etc. This has been solved in many cases by scheduling the chalk talk during the activity period; before commencement of morning classes; during lunch; or during the normal Monday practice period which is shortened to limbering up and a few peppy drills. The school having a complete community enrollment minus bus standards can hold its session at night.

Number of Chalk Sessions

Two chalk talks a week can be sufficient by scheduling one for Monday and one the day before the game. At many small colleges it is normal to hold one skull session on Mondays during the season with the assistant coaches gathering their groups for an hour the morning of a game or on Friday preceding the game. Since these boys are in college for an education primarily it is wise to limit the sessions so as not to conflict with their studies. Too many chalk sessions during the week can have a negative effect upon the morale of your squad. Unexcused absenteeism can create a disciplinary problem for the coaching staff.

Chalk sessions during the season are primarily centered around the dissemination of the scouting report, orientation on the next opponent, and planned strategy for that opponent.

Staff Meetings

Staff meetings have been treated elsewhere and are included in this chapter to re-emphasize their importance as an off-field activity. Daily staff meetings are to be recommended even though some may show little in the way of accomplishment due to the nature of the work being covered or overlapping from the previous meeting. From the standpoint of staff harmony the daily meeting can be highly fruitful. If daily meetings cannot be held, then it is recommended that as many be held as permissible with one a requisite.

Scouting

Scouting is a highly explored off-field activity which can pay off in game winning dividends. The head coach who has the opportunity to scout an opponent and finds excuses not to, but rather, sends an assistant is amiss in his responsibility to his team. Quite often sending an assistant or some layman to scout an opponent is necessitated because of game conflicts. Wherever feasible the head coach and his entire staff should scout the next opponent. Oftentimes when staff members may be assigned to other games, since it may be the only opportunity to observe those teams, or when the coach has no assistants; it is recommended that a friend or two, or a couple of players, or even the wife be taken along and assigned definite spotting duties. At Millersville State College both freshmen coaches do our scouting. They are instructed what to look for and what we want by way of statistics, charts, and diagrams. Whenever a Friday night game is played the entire staff scouts the next opponent the following day.

Assigned Scouting Functions

Responsibilities are assigned to each man, i.e., each freshman coach takes an end on all pass patterns; the line coach watches for line blocking and pulling; the backfield coach watches the man in motion, flanker, slot man, or the swing man; I chart the offensive pattern and get all pertinent information from the assistants. On running plays each assistant checks for blocking, pulling, fakes, etc., and relays the information to me for charting or simply jotting down one of our comparative plays. The same idea extends to defensive spotting.

On Sunday all of this information is sorted out by me and stencils are cut to be mimeographed. Monday morning each assistant coach is given a copy for corrections and study. At the noon staff meeting strategy is mapped out for the opponent and stencils are again run off. At the 7:30 P.M. chalk session a complete mimeographed scouting and strategy report is given to each player. This not only saves time but a clear, concise report with legible diagrams is made available to each player. During the meeting the complete report is covered in detail followed by a question-answer period. The boys are urged to study the report carefully, and it becomes a vital part of the weekly practice program.

The movie of last week's game is screened for game faults and, whenever available, last year's film of the up-coming opponent is studied to supplement the scouting report.

Movies

To the major college coach game films or even practice films, share equal billing in over-all importance with other phases of the football program. Sid Gilman, former coach at Cincinnati University, emphasized this point at a clinic in Newport, Pennsylvania by stating, quote: "I have a wonderful job at Cincinnati, and the only way they can get me to leave this job is to take my film budget from me." Gilman, now coach of San Diego American League professional team, asserted at the time that he even had daily practice movies taken for grading of personnel. The major college coaches use films for evaluation and testing of players' performance. Each player gets a grading at least once weekly and often two or three times. They are tested as though they were in the educational classroom. Of course, such grading is contingent on a staff devoid of teaching duties and a sufficient budget to cover such expenses. Most schools in the minor field could run their entire football program just on the movie budget of these institutions.

There are few schools today which do not film at least one or more of their games. Teaching load and other limitations prohibit an extensive evaluative program. To coaches in this category films can project major faults to players, check offensive and defensive errors, and provide an audio-visual scouting report of your opponent for future years. Few head coaches change their styles from year to year.

At season's end the films can be edited for highlights and used for public relations as well as a teaching aid to show subsequent teams the results of perfection in executing offensive plays and proper defensive alignments.

Charts and Slogans

A few well-chosen charts and slogans can have a positive effect upon the morale as well as the desire for excellence among the team personnel. Quite often these media are over-emphasized resulting in meaningless adornments. They should be selected for the quality of the message, inspirational value, plus example association and exhibited in strategic areas of the locker room and athletic office. For example, one on the door of the locker room, one above the locker room mirror, and one above the coaches' door can suffice for the desired effect upon the team.

Bench Organization

Proper seating of reserve personnel is not only orderly, but it is time-saving for substitution purposes, and allows for easy dissemination of information to related players. Today's rules dictate some efficient method of bench organization for smooth game operation. Some benches, you may at one time or other have observed, created the impression of anarchy within the ranks thus reflecting upon the coach's ability to control his charges in an orderly fashion.

Players should be seated either by position, by squads, or by platoons. Quarterbacks should be strategically seated to be available for information from the players, the coaches, or the spotter's telephone. An assistant coach or a quarterback should be available to handle the telephone, if one is employed by the squad. Players should have full view of the play on the field.

Managers and trainers must be assigned definite bench functions.

Half-Time

Half-time intermission calls for 15 minutes, but actually, at the most, 10 minutes is available; since it takes a minute or two to retreat to the bus or locker room and three minute warm-up period is required before the commencement of the second half. This necessitates a complete minute-by-minute planning of half-time functions. This is a recommended procedure:

Two minutes—toilet relief and trainer care, plus half-time refreshment. Coaches compile errors, etc.

Three minutes—Assistant coaches clarify mistakes individually.

Five minutes—Head coach covers major errors in offensive-defensive play of first half; briefly mentions half-time statistics; recommends strategy changes; suggests possible plays that may hurt opponent's defense; re-emphasize certain plays, answers questions; charts on the board any points for clarification; names second half line-up; and delivers a short pep talk either encouraging or cautioning against laxity and over-confidence.

Post Game Reports

The compiling of offensive-defensive errors and limitations, players' deficiencies, and over-all performance should be jotted down on paper immediately after the game while the information is still fresh in the minds of the staff. This information is invaluable in plotting the practice schedule for the coming week as well as setting up strategy for the next opponent. It brings out the weaknesses of the squad as well as their good points; both vital in planning for the week ahead.

A short staff meeting can be held following the game, or each coach is held responsible for compiling the information and bringing it to the next staff meeting either Sunday or sometimes Monday.

Training Table

The training table poses no problem for the high school coach except possibly during the first two weeks of practice which might entail supervising and planning a menu at a football camp or the noon meal in the school cafeteria. In any case the head coach should either plan the menu or be consulted relative to the meals planned. Most small college coaches are privileged in having training tables for their squads. In some schools he is consulted by the dietician while in others his boys take what they get. The same may be said for the quantity of the meals. Some school dieticians plan for more proteins in the training meal while in other schools the training table is served the same type and same quantity of meal as the regular student body. Such conditions make it rather difficult for the coach to select those foods considered essential in an athlete's diet.

No Cause for Alarm

There is nothing to be alarmed about since many trainers have agreed that a boy should eat any food that does not disagree with him. Most young boys have strong digestive juices and are allergic to few foods. I have had many heavy eaters under my coaching guidance who have dispelled the so-called rules of diet. I can recall a 14-year-old boy at football camp who consumed 18 hot dogs during the lunch period before the cooks cut off his requests for more. This young man underwent a strenuous two hour afternoon practice session in 103 degree weather without showing any ill-effects from over-eating. The above statements are not to be misconstrued as alleging that dietary practices are valueless, but rather to encourage you to make the best of a situation you cannot control.

In situations where the coach can control or recommend the daily diet he should be very careful in planning breakfast and lunch during pre-season practice. A breakfast of juices, cereal with enough milk to moisten, toast, soft-boiled eggs, and fruit is to be recommended. Caution the boys against consuming too much milk since it has a tendency to curdle in the stomach if followed too soon by exerted physical activity. Cold cuts, meat salads, vegetable salads, hot dogs (cooked), peas, string beans, cooked carrots, beets, fruit and ade drinks should constitute the lunch period. The meal should contain nothing heavy and be light. The evening meal should have few restrictions and include plenty of meat and milk. Even desserts including pastries are not frowned upon as they once were. The only check should be maintained upon the heavy boys and a weight reducing diet enforced.

Trips

An itinerary should be prepared for every trip regardless of the distance. It should be mimeographed and handed to each player, or if this is not feasible, it should be posted on the team's bulletin board. The itinerary should include all pertinent information relative to the trip including dress, conduct, seating, deportment while traveling, packing and care of equipment, time of departure, taping time, pre-game meal on distance trips, time to dress, pre-game warm-ups, game time, postgame meal, if any, and departure time plus anticipated home arrival. Few high schools schedule overnight trips while the majority of higher institutions have at least one or more such trips. Caution must be exercised in scheduling activities for the excess free time in the evenings especially with the college boy since there are certain ones who will flaunt training rules. Some coaches take their entire team to a movie, others may hold a chalk session in the evening; however, a safer method is to plan the departure so that arrival will coincide with bedtime.

Statistician

Few coaches realize the motivating value of statistics especially at half-time intermission and during the week in preparation for the up-coming opponent. Think about the type of boy for the job and the method of compiling statistics. Don't overlook the studious boy in the classroom as a prospective statistician. An interested faculty member may well do the job as may some interested alumnus. Other than these people you may have to delegate the function to a manager. Know what statistics you want and mimeograph charts for that purpose.

Today there are excellent scorebooks and statistical books that can serve your purposes. Train your statisticians on how to compile statistics without losing track of the game and resorting to just another game spectator. Wherever feasible have a pair of statisticians as better statistics will be compiled and the responsibility will be lessened on the chief tabulator.

Pep Rallies

Coaches should not minimize the morale values of student pep rallies whether during the school assembly period or an evening bonfire. It displays the school spirit of the student body and develops into a well-rounded esprit de corps. Few players and coaches can sit through a stirring band march without getting the prickly skin feeling and a mental desire to excel for "dear old Siwash." The coach, his staff, and squad including managers, trainers and statisticians should be present ready to contribute in some little way to the celebration. The pep rally is the weekly highlight in the lives of the student body and players short of the game itself. It is at such an occasion that the coach can win over the student population and faculty to football. A carefully prepared talk can accomplish more sometimes than a victory itself. I have seen coaches losing game after game yet retain their stature and prestige in the school environment simply because they took full advantage of the opportunity advanced by the way of the pep rally to cement closer relationships between himself, the staff, the team, and the student body along with the faculty.

Public Relations

A man once made a statement to me which carried quite an impact since I had been receiving more than my share of publicity via newspapers, radio, and television. I was becoming somewhat reluctant and self-conscious feeling I was being overly saturated on the public. He said, "Good publicity never hurts anyone, George." It was well put and I have subscribed to it these many years. There have been many fine articles and books written on the subject of public relations. Bob Walker in his book, *Organization for Successful Football Coaching* (Prentice-

Hall, Inc., Englewood Cliffs, New Jersey, 1960) covers the topic in fine detail.

Every coach has avenue to some media for public relations. Perhaps the simplest yet most convincing is the high school paper. The weekly small town newspaper is hungry for publishable news. I once edited a column in the *Newport News-Sun* titled "The Alibi Corner," which not only brought the town back to high school sports but helped raise $25,500 in a four-year period by means of public subscription and promotions.

A good rule to follow is to do something good and let people know about it whether it be an individual or team accomplishment. Also have something to tell and tell it effectively.

The coach should make himself, his staff and his team an integral part of the community. He should participate in civic affairs and welcome opportunities to speak. Brochures should be available to the press, radio, and television. Cordial and cooperative relations should be maintained with these dispensers of public information as well as students, faculty, administration, school board, clergy, alumni, social organizations, and the public. Every opportunity should be grasped that will promote the welfare of a boy or the team as a whole. Individual honors for the boys are to be discreetly encouraged as they result in prestige for the boy, the team, school, faculty, staff, and the community. Effective publicity has resulted in furthering many boys' higher education. In the same vein sympathetic coverage by fair minded sports writers has saved many a coach's job. The rewards of good public relations are limitless—subscribe to its many tenets.

Morale and Guidance

This topic like public relations deserves attention as an off-field activity. No coach will debate the assertion that team success is contingent upon good team morale. It can be accomplished in many ways such as: public relations, good coaching, coach-player relationship, accomplishment, student-faculty support, community support, proper guidance, and in perhaps many other ways peculiar to individual coaches.

Guidance will direct individual boys into acceptable patterns of behavior. The delinquent or incorrigible boy can be re-directed into better citizenship since football is a means of meeting certain individual needs. It will take sympathy, under-standing, tact, and discretion on the part of a coach which makes the task recommendable for the combined services of other staff members, faculty, guidance counsellor and adminis-trators.

Guidance Relative to College

Boys especially need guidance in the selection of college. Too often the open palm of the athlete is not concerned with his educational background and needs, but rather, is blinded by the monetary rewards offered. We are all cognizant of the mal-practices involved in pressure recruitment. Boys need guidance to be able to discriminate the values of offers in accordance to the educational returns. Every coach should try to help his eligible boys—that is, boys with background educational quali-fications—to earn some form of scholarship or work-aid grant which will enable them to continue their education. The point stressed is that the boy be guided to an institution, whether it be a trade school or a college, that will offer him the most in meeting his educational needs and not over-match him from an athletic standpoint. The oft-quoted phrase, "It is better to be a big fish in a little pond than a little fish in a big pond," con-tains much merit.

Recruiting

In a sense the high school coach carries on a recruiting pro-gram; while there is no question relative to the practice among the college coaching fraternity on all levels whether scholarships are granted or not. The latter coaches will answer letters of alumni, former players, parents and even players. Some visits will be made or campus trips arranged despite the fact there are no inducements to offer the prospective athlete. Many of these college coaches corner prospective-looking athletes on the cam-pus or in gym classes and attempt to sell them on the values of football. Many outstanding athletes have been thus recruited. The high school mentor follows a similar pattern, as he contacts boys in the school environs or gym classes. Many timid or in-decisive boys have been sold on the merits of football, while often the boy is willing but the parents have to be won over. This is recruiting in its narrowest sense. Recruiting must also be accomplished in the junior high school to insure a larger turnout for the team especially among the seventh graders.

Attendance at Games

Few high school coaches are satisfied to remain at home dur-ing the playing season. In many localities the junior high pro-grams commence on Tuesday with jayvee games on Wednesday. In such localities, in order not to conflict with each other, var-sity games are scheduled Thursday, Friday, and Saturday. In such crowded areas a coach can take in at least four games besides his own either as a spectator or a scout. The games may involve his own junior high and jayvee teams or they may be neighboring rivals. In one direction the coach gets a preview of his future players and can evaluate the job his subordinate coaches are doing, while, on the other hand, he can get some insight about his future rivals or detect scouting information. It also affords him an opportunity to observe other coaching techniques, offenses and defenses, strategy, and add possible plays to his repertory. Some of the best plays in many coaches' repertories have been plagiarized from other coaches in this manner. The observant coach can always learn something by being an interested spectator at a game other than his own.

Bulletin Board

The head coach must be responsible for the maintenance of an orderly bulletin board that will contain instruction, rules, charts, statistics, diagrams, pictures, and other pertinent infor-mation related to promoting the welfare and efficiency of the team. A weekly roster should be maintained on the board which must be initialed by each respective player, managers, trainers, statistician and coaching staff including the head coach which will signify that the material has been read by all concerned. Absolute fidelity must be expected in regards to knowing the contents of the board at all times.

Varsity Club

The head coach usually has the added function of acting as advisor to the Varsity Club. This affords him the opportunity of creating a more harmonious atmosphere between the different sports on the school agenda. In many small schools the football coach is also basketball, baseball, or track coach so his influence covers a wider area of pupil participants. Through the Varsity Club the coach can accomplish much in the way of improving a select "esprit de corps" among a segment of the student body which is highly important in instilling pride within the athletes.

SUMMARY

Off-field activities are those that contribute to better field practice routine, more efficient over-all organizational procedure, smoother routine and improved team morale. Each contributes an integral part to the complete team framework with any one having the potential of seriously impeding the desired progress sought-after in the daily workouts. The activities demand complete fidelity to organization and detail mapped out by the head coach and his staff. Managers, trainers, and statisticians relieve the coaching staff of many minute and tedious chores. The chalk session is an efficient way of presenting and distributing important information. Scouting, the bulletin board, and movies supplement vital information needed for evaluation and orientation on opponents. Charts and slogans help build team spirit. Halftime intermissions must be planned for efficient use of limited time while post-game reports keeps vital information fresh for the coming week practice planning. Training tables and trips must be supervised and planned. Pep rallies, the Varsity Club, and public relations contribute to morale and better community spirit plus cooperation. Recruiting must be efficient and is necessary on all levels of competition. Finally, guidance is necessary from the coaching staff to direct the players into proper channels of endeavor, present or future.

11

PROGRAM DURING THE
PLAYING SEASON

Practice Becomes Routine

Once the first game has been played, practice settles down to a routine of staying in top physical condition; keeping that game sharpness; learning the opponent; planning for the opponent; and keeping the team free from injuries. To preserve the latter many coaches abstain from scrimmages trying to accomplish the same results from live drills such as two-on-one, three-on-one, etc. The question of scrimmages is purely one of individual coaching philosophy. There are as many successful coaches in the game today who believe wholeheartedly in scrimmaging at least once or twice weekly as there are those who do not scrimmage once the season begins. Each philosophy has merit, and they both present certain disadvantages which this book will not attempt to cover. Suffice it to say that you will and should follow the principles you know best and believe in most.

For the major college coach every day is a long one of meetings, viewing movies, evaluating personnel, conducting chalk sessions and practice. A 12- to 16-hour day is not unusual. The high school and small college coach have other duties than coaching so the week settles into more or less of a routine affair.

Resumé of a Typical Week

Mondays are light workouts or a day off for certain personnel. The work consists of bags and machine with rough work for

reserve players. With limited squads the rough work is eliminated. Mistakes are corrected and new plays added to offset
scouting done by next opponent. Tuesday is primarily contact
work for remedial purposes. Wednesday is scrimmage day offensive and defensive. Thursday is tapering-off with live drills held
to a minimum. Friday is a review in preparation for the game.

The drills listed in the practice schedule as line drills or backfield drills can be live primarily or merely for timing and sharpness. Remedial work can cover a multitude of things such as
blocking, tackling, timing, steps, pulling, execution of plays,
defensive errors, etc. They are all contingent upon performance
in the last game, glaring weaknesses and probable needs for the
up-coming opponent. Those presented in the following day-by-
day seasonal schedule are listed as refreshers or suggestions since
the needs of each coach will be different although the pattern
will show a resemblance to the outline contained in this
chapter.

Seasonal Practice Program Based Upon
Many Philosophies

The seasonal practice program outlined here for your evaluation has been pieced together after consulting numerous
coaches, reading various articles and books, in addition to many
college publications. The weekly routine is a general plan
which suggests a pattern most coaches can follow. The deficiencies and needs of your team, plus coaching help and time available allows for a certain elasticity in the program to fit the
schedule of most coaches. The plan itself covers a two hour
time allotment with the thought in mind that many coaches
must plan their program on less time. Thus, the time available
to the latter coaches must be reapportioned to best suit their
own particular practice schedule.

Season Weekly Practice Plan

MONDAY—*Light workout* . . . Bags, Machines

3:30–3:45   Practice for early turnouts. . . Specialities for all.
(Major specialists, i.e., punters, kickers, passers, etc.
after practice)

MONDAY—*Light workout* . . . Bags, Machines

3:45–4:00   Calisthenics, agility drills, reaction drills—
            (Referred to in remainder of program as warm-ups)

4:00–4:40	LINE DRILLS	BACK DRILLS
(15 Min-utes)	(a) Stance and starts (b) Pulling for traps (c) Drills for traps and screens (d) Conditioning sprints	(a) Stance and sprints (b) Ball handling (c) Plays (sets)
(15 Min-utes)	(a) Bags—Cross blocking Crab blocking Wedge blocking (b) Bags—By groups thru goal posts under stretched rope to block linebackers and deep secondary in flow of play	(a) Bags—Cross Body blocking, crab blocking, shoulder blocking (b) Two-man sled— Cross body blocking Shoulder blocking Tackling
(10 Min-utes)	(a) Two-man sled— Belly slammers (b) Seven-man sled— Drive	(a) One-on-one pass defense (b) Pass patterns

4:40–4:50   Major mistakes corrected (Last weeks game)
4:50–5:00   Cover opponents offense and strong points by using
            the freshman or jayvee squads.
5:00–5:10   Explain defenses planned for opponent
5:10–5:25   Introduce new plays planned for the next opponent
            and run basic ones against bags. (At least two new
            plays should be added to your repertory.)
5:25–5:30   Sprints, dashes or 880 run (For conditioning pur-
            poses.)
5:30–   Specialists program and individual remedial in-
            struction

TUESDAY—*Contact Work* (2-on-1, 3-on-1, etc.)

3:30–3:45   Practice for early turnouts . . . Specialities
3:45–4:00   Warm-ups

4:00–4:45	LINE DRILLS	BACK DRILLS
(20 Minutes)	(a) Seven-man sled— shiv, roll-outs (b) Staggered signals line charges (c) One-on-one (d) Two-on-one	(a) Stance and sprint (b) Ball-handling (c) Plays (sets) (d) Pass patterns
(25 Minutes)	(a) Three-on-one (b) Five-on-two (c) Whole line	(a) Two-man sled— Blocking, Tackling (b) Live Circle blocking drill (c) Two on one open field blocking-tackling drill

4:45–5:00	Punt and P.A.T. scrimmage
5:00–5:15	Pass scrimmage—Forming pocket patterns, defense
5:15–5:25	Live tackling and blocking drills—Gauntlet, circle, sideline three on three, pursuit or scrimmage new plays
5:25–5:30	Sprints, dashes or 880 run
5:30–	Specialists or remedial work

Note: The three on one and five on two drills are the Oklahoma drills which covers one on one, two on one, trapping, pulling, wedging and forming the pass pocket. The full line drills cover traps, wedging, hole blocking, protecting the passer, etc. The backfield drill, "two on one open field," refers to a ball-carrier, a blocker and a deep defensive secondary man (about 10 yards). It is a live ball carrying, blocking-tackling drill.

(Jayvees continue to ready opponents plays for scrimmage)

WEDNESDAY—*Scrimmage Day*

3:30–3:45	Practice for early turnouts. . . Specialities
3:45–4:00	Warm-ups
4:00–4:45	Defensive scrimmage against opponents plays as run by frosh or jayvee teams. Offensive team can observe (in case some are used defensively) or run plays against dummies.

WEDNESDAY—*Scrimmage Day*

4:45–5:30	Offensive scrimmage against jayvees or frosh teams using opponents defenses or against own defensive platoon
5:30–	Conditioning running and specialists

Note: Some coaches substitute contact drills for scrimmage

THURSDAY—*Tapering-Off Work*

3:30–3:45	Practice for early turnouts. . . Specialties
3:45–4:00	Warm-ups
4:00–4:25	Review opponents offense (with aid of frosh or jay-teams). Check their best plays again. Cover defenses to be used and review all position responsibilities and cautions.
4:25–4:45	Run goal line plays aganst dummies (6, 7, 8-man lines). Use live scrimmage (controlled) if necessitated
4:45–5:00	Run bread and butter and special (trick) plays against dummies simulating opponents defenses
5:00–5:15	Pass patterns especially new ones and spreads
5:15–5:30	Review punt plays, P.A.T. plays, quick kicks and any quick kick plays
5:30–	Conditioning runs and specialists

FRIDAY—*General Review*

3:30–3:45	Practice for early turnouts. . . Specialities
3:45–4:00	Warm-ups
4:00–4:15	Review opponent again offensively and defensively Little pep talk . . . motivates remainder of practice
4:15–4:30	Kick-offs. . . Runbacks with proper blocking functions, coverage. Punts . . . Coverage, protection, and daisy-chain return (double safety)
4:30–5:25	Run through all offensive plays—either triangle style or by charging up and down the field
5:25–5:30	Last minute instructions; one fast dash; short workout for the specialists
7:00 P.M.	Chalk talk and movies if needed

SATURDAY—*Game Preparations* (Trip itinerary when away game)

10:00 . . .	Line-backfield meeting
11:00 . . .	Pre-game meal
11:30 . . .	Taping
1:30 . . .	Pre-game warm-ups:

      (a) Calisthenics and grass drills

      (b) *Linemen:* Charges, pulling, shiving on each other, half-speed one on one or bumping shoulders, huddle and break, punt coverage, specialities

      (c) *Backs:* Sprints, receiving punts, punting, kick-offs, passing and receiving

      (d) By teams run up and down field with QB handing off ball to backs on straight dives to get feel of game and field

1:50 . . .	Retire to dressing room for last minute repairs, taping changes instructions and brief pep talk
1:57 . . .	Return to field for game
2:00 . . .	On to victory

SUMMARY

Pre-season practice is a hectic merry-go-round from morning until dusk with sweat, aching muscles, work, drive-drive, optimism or pessimism. Once the first game has been played the brunt of the work has been accomplished. Practice eases off into a routine that finds a coaching staff trying to keep their squad in peak physical condition; maintaining game sharpness; polishing for poise and confidence; moulding the inexperienced team to reach peak capacity as quickly as possible; scouting the opponents—studying their strengths and weaknesses; planning game strategy; nurturing team morale and staff harmony; and maintaining a cooperative liaison within the school and community.

Each practice day involves a special program which is based upon the deficiencies of the squad, work necessitated by the opponent and the special philosophy plus strategy of the coach and his staff. The day varies in time element from early morning to late at night for the major college staff to a matter of limited time for the small college coach and their high school coaches with teaching functions. Each session is determined by the philosophy of the head coach which determines the amount of contact work, scrimmage or other type, that will be included in the weekly work. In the main, the work will generate into a routine that will pretty much dictate light workouts, if any, on Mondays; remedial work based upon contact slated for Tuesdays; scrimmage or heavy contact drills on Wednesdays; tapering-off work with some remedial and contact drills on Thursdays; and a full review of opponent and own strategy plus all offensive plays on Fridays. Chalk sessions are held every day by many major college coaches to a minimum one or two by the small college and high school coaches. The work is planned on a weekly basis along a more or less routine pattern.

12

SPRING PRACTICE

Not Common to All Schools

There are some state athletic associations which permit spring practice for high schools; however, the majority have restrictions against such programs. The major colleges, outside of a few conferences such as the Ivy League, feel that a spring football program is an absolute necessity in promoting a better brand of fall football excellence. On the one hand, it is viewed as over-emphasis while on the other hand it is deemed as not only desirable but a necessity. Small colleges are split on the program; some having a full program; others a modified program; and still others no program at all. There is no question that positive results are the advantages of such a program. It actually is a program of experimentation and development without the fear of impeding injuries.

Wide Areas of Work Covered

No definite program can be drawn up for spring practice since the whole program is predicated on experimentation based upon some definite area of individual team needs. Some coaches may spend the entire spring working on defense; others may work on offense or experiment with new systems; while others may work strictly on fundamentals or individual drills.

Theory

Many coaches hold to the theory that football teams are made in the spring. They feel that there is no soft way to become a football player, because the game involves blocking and tackling which cannot be taught on the blackboard. The game is not all Saturday afternoon glamor but hours of physical contact, sweat, sacrifice, and drill on the practice field. You knock down; and you get knocked down; and sometimes it hurts hard. Spring practice is just this type of football—violent, body-bruising workouts, knocking heads and devoid of any glamor; since coaches can sacrifice injuries in spring practice. This is the period when intestinal fortitude is established.

The Content of Spring Practice Is Evaluation

Fall practice is mostly aimed at polishing, perfecting, and preparing for each weekly opponent. Spring practice allows the coach to observe each individual boy especially those coming up from the jayvee team or the college freshman team. This is a serious time for these boys, because their performance will determine to a great degree whether or not they will fit into the team's fall plans. Spring practice also affords various staff coaches opportunities to correct varying weaknesses in veteran players. Players are shifted around to other positions in an effort to find out whether they can be of more value to themselves and the team. Often a loophole is greatly strengthened by such experimentation. For example, a big fullback may not have the agility or speed required for that position yet he could make a good guard or defensive linebacker.

Establishes Team Unity

Spring practice helps establish unity as a team, especially since this may be a period when you will get new boys to come out for the squad. The college freshmen and transfer students sitting out a year of ineligibility are now vying for positions along with returning veterans. They now are afforded an opportunity to get acquainted with each other more or less family style. The end result is a harmonious team with one common goal—team success. The high school coach with restrictions on spring practice can accomplish many of these goals in physical education classes.

Day by Day Proposition in Most Schools

In trying to present a definite spring practice program for the readers several major college coaches were consulted with the purpose of soliciting part or all of their practice schedule for presentation in this book. It was surprising to learn that no weekly or complete spring practice plan was pre-drawn prior to the time of practice. While old ones were on file, most programs were planned on a day-to-day basis. Rip Engle has old forms on file and draws from his fall schedules. With the help of his staff, he makes additions and deletions in drawing up a new practice schedule on a day-to-day or weekly basis depending upon goals set up for the spring practice. The daily program is mimeographed and distributed to each member of his staff. Penn State concludes its four week (20-day) program with a full scale scrimmage between Blue and White teams as a feature of their two day football clinic held annually for high school and college coaches.

The Michigan State Spring Practice Philosophy

Another coach consulted was Hugh "Duffy" Daugherty, coach of Michigan State University, and an old hometown friend. The author felt certain he could obtain the Michigan State schedule because of the old relationship. It came as somewhat of a surprise when Duffy explained that Michigan State did not hold to a definite, pre-drawn spring practice program but rather planned their practices on a day-by-day basis. According to Duffy, the staff would meet every day prior to practice at which time the practice agenda would be planned. Each coach would offer suggestions based upon the needs and performances of his delegated charges. Duffy would offer his over-all views and the objectives he felt should be achieved. From this point the practice program would be pieced together to accomplish the desired goals. Each assistant coach jotted his functions for the afternoon on his clipboard and the daily work was in outline form. Daugherty added that the plan was very elastic to allow for improvisation on the field whenever the occasion demanded. He concluded by stating that on many occasions he would start practice according to the planned schedule then refute the whole plan by throwing the teams into a good bang up scrimmage. He intimated that although spring practice is designed to accomplish certain objectives based upon experimentation and contact work it is difficult to pinpoint the work to specific details on paper. Spring practice is, or can be, the toughest practice in football; and it can materialize into a chore bordering upon drudgery. A coach must be alert to read the signs among his players. Players lose their enthusiasm and eventually start hating spring practice. Throwing the script out of the window at times when signs of monotony and listless performance appear is using discretion that will pay-off in better results and higher team morale. Work must be the order of practice but a certain amount of work-fun can also be inter-mixed to improve over-all efficiency.

Some Coaches Stress Fundamentals Primarily

A few years ago at the National Football Clinic held annually in Atlantic City, New Jersey, I was trying to get spring practice ideas to supplement our newly instigated spring program at Millersville. The recommendations offered were many and varied. Quite a few coaches emphasized their own individual theories that fundamentals of the game should be stressed primarily. Their contention was that many of the finer details, those little techniques, were either overlooked in the fall practice or were covered hastily because of the short interval of time available before the opening game. Spring practice was, according to them, the ideal time to stress every phase of fundamentals from stance, steps, to actual blocking and tackling. When questioned, Bill Meek, one of the clinicians and head coach at Southern Methodist University, informed the writer that he did not make use of the scrimmage to any degree; but he did utilize various drills to teach fundamentals peculiar to his offense and defense.

Calendar Time for Spring Practice

The question relative to the time of spring most feasible to hold spring practice is dependent upon many factors. In many schools football players are not permitted to engage in spring sports so the coach may select twenty days in the best of spring weather and extend them over five or six weeks by practicing four days weekly and making up missed sessions due to inclement weather. Some coaches can realize only fifteen days of workouts due to spring conflicts. The major colleges, in northern states especially, usually start the first week of April and conclude drills the first week-end of May. Southern colleges normally drill during the month of March although some practice earlier. Many small college coaches, even in northern states, start practice in February and finish during early March. By staging their sessions at this time they are able to get their whole squad out for the drills, since spring practice for baseball, track, etc., will just be getting under way. Of course, the weather is highly unpredictable at this time of the year and the workouts will be hindered to a degree. However, as one coach said, it was either this or forget spring practice since there would not be enough players out for practice to make it worthwhile. The small college football player usually has the talent for more than one sport, and the lack of competition by numbers in the other sports opens the avenue for participation on other athletic teams. The matter of time then is wholly dependent upon your own local situation and the problems it presents. The most feasible time from the weather standpoint is the month of April when the days are still moderately cool and rain not too continuous but more of the shower type. April does not interfere with mid-semester or semester examinations.

Planning the Practice Schedule

Earlier in this chapter it was stated that no definite season day-by-day practice program could be pre-drawn since no two teams will be aiming for the same objectives. Personnel, graduation losses, new recruits, experience of squad, position weakness, need for experimentation, etc. will determine the planning of the schedule which almost dictates a day-to-day plan. In view of these facts the recommendation is made that you select a definite area of team need and build your practice schedule to fulfill those requirements. To do this you will have to draw upon your fall program as a supplement to provide needed drills and a general outline to follow. Perhaps the following experience may serve as a suggestion. The first spring Millersville initiated spring practice two-thirds of the practice was devoted to basic fundamentals and the remaining third to offensive and defensive work with as much scrimmage as time and general physical condition would allow. An intra-squad scrimmage climaxed the spring practice. The following year we switched from the balanced line multiple offense to an unbalanced line multiple slot offense. The complete spring program was utilized in experimenting and perfecting the new offense. The scrimmage was used to a great extent. The past spring involved a more or less balanced program with perhaps some emphasis on the single wing which offered great potential as a supplement to the T-variations in our offensive repertory.

The importance of spring practice can be pointed out by our own experience at Millersville State College. Prior to spring workouts we had won 11 games, lost 20, tied one. With the inauguration of spring practice the record shows four consecutive winning seasons and a 22-13 over-all record.

Balanced Spring Practice Program

If you are satisfied with your general offensive-defensive repertory, your graduation losses are normal and your squad experience is average or better then a balanced spring practice program is recommended. Such a plan would involve a four week program that would cover four major phases of football. The practice plan itself can be pre-planned and pre-drawn by consulting your fall pre-season program and combining both morning and afternoon sessions into one cohesive session that will adopt the best features of both practices. The first week would involve conditioning despite the fact that sweatsuits were probably issued a month earlier for running purposes. The core of the second week would center around fundamentals, and the third and fourth weeks would emphasize the offensive-defensive strategy of the head coach. Naturally there will be much over-lapping of the different phases because you cannot separate offensive or defensive drills from conditioning or fundamentals as you cannot separate the latter from the former. The phases of work are separated by emphasis only. Because of its motivating incentive a full-scale intra-squad scrimmage should climax the spring program. The following four week program is a summary or brief outline of a suggested balanced spring practice plan. The details should be filled in from your fall program.

First Week:

    CONDITIONING — Calisthenics, Agility Drills, Reaction Drills, Running, Bags and Machines, Formations—Offensive plays. Stances.

Second Week:

    FUNDAMENTALS — Individual Drills, Mass Contact Drills (Blocking and Tackling), Defensive Alignments (In combination with offensive plays).

Third Week:

    EMPHASIZE OFFENSE—Cover the Kicking Game, The Passing Game, The Running Game, And Add or Expand Your Offense on an Experimental Basis (Try some spread plays for example). Scrimmage as much as possible.

Fourth Week:

    EMPHASIZE DEFENSE—Teach New Defenses, Variations, And Perfect Old Ones. Again use the scrimmage as much as possible.

Intra-Squad Scrimmage: Break up the teams to bring about the best balance possible for the scrimmage. Emphasize sportsmanship as tempers may flare.

SUMMARY

Spring practice while not common to most high schools and many small colleges is an integral part of the majority of major college programs and understandably so in view of the competitive stress found on these levels. It is a program that can be based upon many areas of the total football picture such as fundamentals, remedial work on an individual basis, experimentation and over-all perfecting of the total offense and defense. Programs will vary with different schools because the needs and objectives of each squad are dependent upon many factors peculiar to the local situation. The programs may involve fundamentals with contingent drills to a maximum of scrimmage since the philosophies of the many coaches involved range in theories. Many feel that it is a time calling for complete contact work where the men will be separated from the boys, where intestinal fortitude is established, and injuries cannot influence the outcome of an upcoming game since sufficient time is available for convalescence. It is a time to experiment at the different position levels, with different players, new offensive-defensive theories, and learn about the players by more closer inspection plus contact. The work can be accelerated at any pace required by the progress of the team. And finally the content of the needs or goals to be realized and achieved almost dictate a spring practice schedule predicated upon a day-to-day basis. In those cases where the returning squad poses few problems of graduation losses, inexperience, etc., a balanced spring practice program is recommended with a suggested outline contained in the chapter.

13

INTEGRATION OF PRACTICE SCHEDULES

Areas of Similarity

A close check of the six pre-season practice schedules presented in this book will show very little variance except for terminology and emphasis on certain areas of training. From the letter to the parents, and to the boys themselves, the schedules follow a line of almost complete similarity; starting with the first week based almost exclusively upon a phase devoted to conditioning and fundamentals; through a second week of establishing the framework of the game itself wherein offense-defense and placement of personnel get the chief attention by way of drills and scrimmage; and a final week of orientation towards the first opponent with perfection of timing and reaching that game sharpness which is the culmination of the three weeks of training.

Areas of similarity in all six schedules can be found in the conditioning phases at the beginning of practice where some form of warm-up consists of calisthenics, grass drills, agility drills and reaction drills teamed with running in one form or another such as sprints and dashes. In addition, some form of conditioning is utilized at the close of practice. A chalk session with its dependent football manual is a part of each program, and drills involving some phase of the kicking game and passing game receive attention during the first week of practice. Despite individual fundamentals all six schedules begin offensive teaching of basic plays during the first week with some attention also devoted to the defensive game. All schedules emphasize the basic ingredients of the game; namely, blocking and tackling throughout the first and second week.

All six schedules pinpointed ball-handling drills and foot-work for the backs while, at the same time, teaching drills to linemen which stressed footwork and speed in getting to the point of attack. Linemen in particular received more contact drills due to the nature of their positions than the backs who by necessity had a wider variety of drills to master. Pursuit drills were stressed along with pass defense drills, each being a vital supplement to defenses being taught. All coaches adhered to a policy of training relative to teaching plays by the use of dummies set up in various defenses; thus, each coach recognized the importance of teaching blocking to meet changing multiple defenses.

The schedules, especially those on the junior high school, senior high school, and the small college level, offered some form of remedial work during the middle of the second week.

Stances and starts were stressed quite emphatically in all six practice programs during the first week with special attention devoted to the snap count and exchange on the university level. The kicking game in all of its component parts received much attention by all schools involved.

Scrimmage

The use of the scrimmage as a motivating device in addition to its major function as a method of evaluation shows areas of similarity and some divergence. All six schools used it rather extensively until the third week in perfecting offenses and de-fenses and as a means of personnel selection. Inter-school scrim-mages during the second week of practice were evident even though not openly listed, as it is a common practice at a major-ity of the schools throughout the United States today. For example, while Penn State did not list a scrimmage game on the schedule, such a game has been held in the past against Bucknell University. The author is sure the Air Force Academy tests its charges against an outside college, because NCAA rules allow such a practice within limits; and the scrimmage game offers so many advantages concomitant to early season training.

Difference in scrimmage philosophy, and understandably so, were found in the junior high school and small high school where this evaluative-teaching device was not used until the second week. The large high school and colleges resorted to the scrimmage during the first week. Millersville had their first full-scale scrimmage on Saturday, the sixth day; Air Force Academy scrimmaged lightly the second day and all-out on Saturday, the sixth day; Penn State had rough work on the second day and, like the Air Force Academy, a full scrimmage on the sixth day, Saturday. Full scrimmages were engaged in by Penn State on Wednesday and Saturday of the second week. This was identical to Millersville, Highlands, Johnstown, Cherrytree-Newport, John Reynolds Junior High School, and I feel sure Air Force Academy. It was brought out in the larger school sessions that live contact work was stressed every day during the first two weeks in drills or scrimmage.

Wherever feasible—that is, depending on number of personnel making up the squads—jayvees were used in orienting the varsity squads during the third week of practice relative to the first opponents offensive-defensive patterns. Post pre-season practice seems to be of an identical nature in the six schools involved thus summing up areas of similarity.

Areas of Difference

There are areas of differences in the six schedules presented which can be accounted for by cognizance of personnel, experience, staff, and time. The Academy schedule is highly accelerated mainly because only one period per day is available and that does not constitute two hours. As a result, game conditions must be stressed as early as possible at the possible expense of valuable drills teaching fundamentals, with the whole practice program initiating live contact work as early as the first day. In a similar way Penn State goes into live contact work early in the week. The first live contact work in the junior high program comes in the form of a light blocking workout during the fifth day. The same holds true for the small high school where one-on-one and two-on-one drills are first utilized on Friday, the fifth day. This is understandable since both programs are based upon the assumption the kids are all inexperienced and must be taught from the barest fundamentals to ultimate game efficiency. It is a program predicated upon slow teaching in the early stages with patience and repetition based upon attention to detail and mastery.

Sam Thompson in his John Reynolds program advocated mass drills because he believes he can reach more boys. The philosophy has merit as many coaches prefer such drills rather than having boys standing idly by.

The Cherrytree-Newport schedule builds up to the full scrimmage with a modified five-man and eight-man scrimmage which utilizes center-passing, running, blocking and tackling. It also introduces circle blocking and circle tackling which are mass drills that accomplish the desired fundamentals with an economy of time.

The Highlands and Johnstown High School programs get into heavy work, quickly engaging in as many scrimmages and as much live work as the other five schools.

The Millersville State College practice program can be somewhat termed a liaison program between the public schools and the universities as it encompasses most of the features of the high schools with acceleration towards more specialization which is related to the university program. It can be readily adopted by most high schools and easily adjusted to adopt the main features of the university program.

The university program's main difference can be reiterated in the summation that it involves more organization, supervision, time, and specialization. Of course, in essence, this is the keynote of all six organized practice schedules.

Drills

It would be virtually impossible to select and explain all of the drills constituting each practice program, since such a venture could embody a complete book in itself. On close inspection it will be noticed that, in the main, most of the drills listed in the different schedules are similar. Of course, the drills listed under the Penn State program may differ not only in terminology but also in content, which can be accounted for by more detailed position specialization as well as group work aided and abetted by a larger coaching staff to meet the proficiency demanded in the major college field. The majority of the drills, too, are self-explanatory.

It may be appropriate to advise a coach drawing up a schedule from those listed in this book to adopt only those drills that will fit in with his own scheme of teaching. You are familiar with your own drills, and by sticking to known drills you will produce more positive results in your coaching. The schedules listed in this book can act as a guide, especially to the novice coach, by indicating where drills of his own choosing should be inserted in the conditioning phase; individual fundamentals such as pulling, charging, steps, etc.; the offensive development involving plays, kicking, passing, and blocking; and finally the defensive game. Where a new idea appears by way of developing his own plans or a new drill will fit into his methods, then he is urged to incorporate all features of the six schedules presented in this book which will supplement his own program.

Conclusions

Many conclusions could be arrived at by close study of the contents and organization of each schedule presented in this book. This book was written to allow the many football coaches at large to study and compare ideas incorporated on the various levels of the football echelon based upon a geographical sampling of different competitive levels among several states and their methods of teaching the game. It must be concluded that each program is peculiar to the school involved and as such can be an example of all schools on its representative level. Any differences will not be in content and organization as much as in philosophy and allowances or limitations on the coach and his staff. The schedules are admittedly elastic for improvisation, additions or deletions. Other schedules on a comparative level may offer more variety or a different apportionment of time, but it is doubtful that any can show a wide divergence of content. It may also be true that some coaches would be prone to an easier pace during the first week of practice, and would stress fundamentals on an individual basis rather than push into full team contact as is evidenced in the enclosed practice programs. However, the enormity of today's game and early game schedules mandate an accelerated program of practice. Too, it may be concluded that perhaps a morning session of a maximum of one hour devoted to conditioning and execution of plays for timing and finesse in shorts could be substituted in the junior high program. The afternoon session limited to ninety minutes could be devoted to game fundamentals under contact conditions. Thus a two and one-half hour program broken down into two sessions would not over-tax the physical stamina or be a detriment to the health of the boys yet create a more wholesome teaching-learning atmosphere.

The schedules presented in this book through the courtesy and cooperation of the contributing coaches are well organized and closely integrated to produce the desired results on their comparative levels. They may not be the best examples on their representative levels but they can serve as models for guidance purposes and are based upon backgrounds of outstanding success.

Perhaps one recommendation may be offered as a concluding study of the different programs, yet it may not be feasible under certain school conditions. With the admissible cry of more time needed to get ready perhaps a mandated four week pre-season practice rule is needed for better first game preparation. The recommendation offers both advantages and disadvantages, which will not be expanded here, with the advantages outweighing the disadvantages from the standpoint of readiness.

Results

Results of the different programs can only be compared from the outcome of seasonal schedules. At the time these schedules were submitted Air Force Academy had completed an undefeated season and an engagement in the Cotton Bowl; Penn State has made two successful trips to the Liberty Bowl; John Reynolds Junior High School completed an undefeated season; Newport Joint High School had run up 17 straight victories;

Millersville State College just completed its fourth consecutive winning season with a 6-3 record; Johnstown High School finished undefeated; and Highlands High School had an undefeated ledger. These results must attest to the validity of good organization, methods of teaching and contents of the programs presented. Yet, these results must not be accepted as all-conclusive. Had the above-listed teams gone from the heights to the bottom of the success ladder there would be no criteria for evaluating the complete results of each program because you cannot measure the effectiveness of these programs on paper due to the many intangibles involved. Only the people directly involved can see, can feel, and can measure the results of any program involving a winning or losing team. Quite often better methods and better teaching is involved in losing causes. These are the intangibles that do not show up in the results.

The How-to

No definite hard and fast rule can be prescribed for you in showing you, or the beginning coach, how to administer your program. Methods on the "How-to" must be based in large part on your individual background, your methods of teaching, your philosophy of the game, and as much of the routine of your high school and college coaches which you have learned well and which you accept. The veteran coach is well entrenched in his methods of teaching, his staff organization, and his practice content and routine. The beginning coach may get many valuable suggestions out of the many programs offered in this book. Points in any of the practice plans that may be vague in meaning can easily be clarified by a letter to any of the coaches in question. Even the veteran coach may pick up an idea or two from the contents of this book with regards to the "How-to" of organization and administration of the complete practice program. It is comparable to attendance at a football clinic where everything appears elementary until suddenly something new is brought to the horizon and the clinic becomes worthwhile. Do not change any successful style of presenting (the How-to) your program to your charges but scrutinize this book for that possible clinical new idea that may strengthen your style. The unsuccessful coach or the struggling coach with mediocre average success may well need a complete analysis of his methods and program and may find some answers in this book. The beginning coach cannot help benefiting from a study of this book. It will help him to establish his "How-to" in drawing up his program, organization, and teaching. All the component parts of the football game must be a part of his program. If he plans well, it should be apparent at season's end in the won-lost record.

INDEX

INDEX